EASY THAI

An Introduction to the Thai Language

EASY THAI

An Introduction to the Thai Language

with Exercises and Answer Key.
A Gradual and Cumulative System
with Little Time Wasted.

by GORDON H. ALLISON

CHARLES E. TUTTLE COMPANY
Rutland, Vermont & Tokyo, Japan

Published by the Charles E. Tuttle Company, Inc.
an imprint of Periplus Editions (HK) Ltd.

© 1969 by Charles E. Tuttle Co., Inc.

First Tuttle edition, 1969
Twenty-seventh printing, 1999

Printed in Singapore

Distribution:

North America
Tuttle Publishing
Distribution Center
Airport Industrial Park
364 Innovation Drive
North Clarendon, VT 05759-9436
Tel: (802) 773-8930
Tel: (800) 526-2778

Japan
Tuttle Publishing
RK Building 2nd Floor
2-13-10 Shimo-Meguro, Meguro-Ku
Tokyo 153 0064
Tel: (03) 5437-0171
Fax: (03) 5437-0755

Asia Pacific
Berkeley Books Pte Ltd.
5 Little Road #08-01
Singapore 536983
Tel: (65) 280-1330
Fax: (65) 280-6290

TABLE OF CONTENTS

RAPID THAI

PUBLISHER'S FOREWORD

Learning Thai through the medium of this introduction to the language is like learning to swim the easy way, entering where the water is not deep and under the watchful eye of a competent instructor—not taking a sudden plunge or push into the mysterious depths where the shock may be so great as to dissuade the beginner from ever again trying.

Easy Thai is a painless and comparatively easy way of swimming in a language spoken by 30 million Thais. It is a lovely language, indigenous to a lovely country that is also one of the leading tourist meccas of the world and a favorite Rest and Recreation spot for GI's.

This is a gradual and cumulative system of learning the 44 Thai consonants and the 32 basic vowels that make up the alphabet. Eventually, like a jigsaw puzzle, the pieces (sounds, tones, letters) fall into place and make sense—and a new world of pleasurable attainment has opened up.

The publisher heartily recommends this pleasure and is proud to make the book available to those who like and accept challenges.

FOREWORD

The primary objective of this modest little book is to whet the interest of the reader enough to go on with his study of the Thai language. We have tried to introduce you to some of the "mysteries" of Thai as painlessly but as rapidly as we thought practicable.

There seems to be a great deal of misunderstanding among non-Thai-speaking foreigners about the Thai language and its place in the world—or even its place in Thailand! Let us assure you, however, that the Thai language is a rich and useful language and becoming more so every day. The time you spend in learning Thai will not be wasted. Perhaps you will one day even agree with us, to the effect that the more one learns about Thai, the more he realizes what a remarkable language it really is and the more he wants to learn about it.

Though the people of Thailand are naturally very interested, by and large, in English and other widely-used languages, let no one jump to the mistaken conclusion that they do not love their own language. They do, very much, and perhaps because of this great affection they have for it, they like to hear it spoken to a somewhat broader extent than simply "Come here!", "Go home!", etc.

Real Thai is a very colorful, expressive language indeed, and we sincerely hope that you will have the opportunity to appreciate this fact for yourself, with your own ears and through your own understanding.

We make no presumptuous claims about the academic value of this little volume. It is not designed to be a scholarly work but only to be used as a tool or a stepping-stone to something much more worthwhile.

G. H. A.

Faculty of Political Science
Thammasat University, Bangkok

INTRODUCTION

"The Linguist" Magazine of Bangkok, Thailand, has honored us by requesting us to prepare some lessons on the Thai language that might be interesting to foreigners (non-Thais, that is) both in Thailand and abroad. We are pleased to try, but first we should like to make a few introductory remarks about Thailand and the Thai language, just in case you may not already be familiar with this lovely country and its beautiful language.

Thailand and the Thai language are becoming better and better known around the world. Whereas, before World War II and perhaps even as recently as ten years ago, the Thai language was generally regarded by most Westerners as a "rare" or "exotic" —even "mysterious"—language, it is now taking its place among the ranks of the useful modern languages. No longer is it considered rather unusual to find a "Westerner" who can not only speak Thai but can also read and write it. This is as it should be because the Thai language is a rich and distinctive one, well worth the trouble of learning.

Besides being spoken by at least thirty million people in Thailand, the Thai language is undoubtedly known by a great number of people in many other countries, not only in Southeast Asia but all over the world. As for those areas outside the geographical confines of Thailand where the Thai language or a dialect of standard Thai may be heard, we could mention the Shan States in Burma, many parts of Laos, parts of Yunnan Province in China, parts of Cambodia, and even in Canton province in China! (Although the Lao language is itself considered as a separate language and not a dialect of Thai—it is true—you will find that practically speaking it is an older, more-orthographically-simple form of Thai that is relatively easy to learn for anyone who knows the Thai language to begin with.)

The country of Thailand itself has indeed become more and more famous in recent times for various practical reasons and because of many famous Thai personages themselves. Bangkok, the capital, is becoming year by year ever more a center of international activities and a must on the itinerary of tourists visiting Asia. But in spite of all this internationalization admittedly going on in Bangkok, there remain the traditional charm and friendliness of the Thai people and the romantic appeal of a charming land.

We sincerely hope all readers will one day have the opportunity to experience first-hand the interesting and delightful new world that will be yours in Thailand, particularly if you know something of the Thai language. If these modest lessons can help you to learn and use the Thai language profitably and pleasurably, we will feel gratified and honored indeed.

As for the lessons themselves, we plan to move as quickly as possible and to give you useful words (actually written in Thai, which you can easily learn to read if you will simply follow our lessons slowly but surely) as quickly as possible also. The first few lessons may be too slow to suit your taste, and some of the words used are admittedly not the most-useful ones. However, if you will stick with us, we believe we can assure you that after a few lessons you will be reading, using, and understanding many useful Thai words and phrases.

The lessons will be cumulative, with up-to-date lists from time to time of what we have already taught you in previous lessons. And in later lessons we will also give you complete lists of Thai consonants, vowels, and the phonetic system we employ to show Thai sounds in English letters, as well as other material we consider useful to persons interested in learning the Thai glanuage.

Each lesson will be accompanied by exercises making use of the material presented in that lesson (plus material presented in previous lessons, to some extent). You should try to do the exercises yourself, without looking at the "Answers" also given in the same lesson. If you will use the lessons as reference material, then you should have no trouble doing all the exercises yourself before checking the "Answers". As for writing the Thai letters themselves, it will help you to remember them if you will attempt to write them at least once or twice in doing the exercises. Don't worry so much about how your written letters look. No one writes nice-looking Thai letters from the beginning (at least no one we've ever seen). Actually, you will be "printing" your Thai letters—not "writing" them—but that is normal practice in Thai for most people. Good luck!

G.H.A.

Bangkok, Thailand.

NOTE FOR 2nd PRINTING, 1st EDITION

It was our intention to revise this book for the 2nd edition. However, it has proved to be popular the way it is and we have learned from experience that it is sometimes best to "leave well enough alone". Therefore, most of the work we did for the 2nd edition of this book will appear—soon, hopefully—in the form of "Easy Spoken Thai". The only changes we have made in this second printing are very minor ones. We have not changed our basic system of phonetics, as it has proved to be a popular one for people just getting acquainted with the Thai language. It is of course obvious that our phonetic system as used in this book is not for the scholars or the experts—it is only the "means to an end".

G. H. A.

Professional Services
Bangkok, Thailand
February 1968

NOTE FOR 3rd PRINTING, 1st EDITION

We have nothing much to add at this time, except "Thank you", for our many customers who agree with us that the Thai language is well worth a little time and effort spent in learning something about it. For this new printing, we have made additional minor changes, with the objective, simply, of improving the book a bit for our customers and readers.

G. H. A.

Professional Services
Bangkok, Thailand
July 1968

LESSON 1

THE MOST-IMPORTANT LOW-CLASS CONSONANTS

$$(\text{ค}, \text{ง}, \text{ช}, \text{ซ}, \text{ญ})$$

Introduction. Thai consonants and vowels are considered separately and are governed by different rules. We plan to introduce such matters to you gradually. The first thing you should he aware of is that Thai consonants number 44 altogether and are divided into three groups:—

        (1) 24 low—class consonants;

        (2)   9 middle—class consonants;

        (3) 11 high--class consonants.

You may wonder why there should be such distinctions between consonants of the same alphabet (the Thai alphabet), but you will understand later on when you learn something about tones. For the time being simply try to learn the consonants gradually, as they are introduced, keeping in mind whether they are low-class, middle-class, or high-class consonants. Do not concern yourself about the tonal distinctions and rules at the beginning of your study of Thai.

Table No. 1   Low—Class Consonants

Note. These consonants are listed in Thai alphabetical order, in order gradually to accustom you to the dictionary order of Thai words. (However, we do not start at the beginning of the Thai alphabet, since the beginning consonants of the Thai alphabet are more difficult in certain ways.) To help you remember the Thai alphabetical order of consonants, therefore, we use a certain number for each consonant. This number shows the numerical order of that consonant in the entire 44–consonant Thai alphabet. If you will get in the habit, at the beginning of your study of Thai, of associating each consonant with the number we give for it, you will find it much easier to learn the entire Thai alphabet later on, and your use of Thai dictionaries will then be much facilitated.

Low–Class Consonant	Numerical order in Thai Alphabet	Name of the Consonant in English Phonetics	Equivalent Sound in English
ค	4	KAW	K
ง	7	NGAW	NG
ช	10	CHAW	CH
ซ	11	SAW	S
ญ	13	YAW YEENG	Y

Notes. 1) Try writing each Thai consonant yourself a few times. This will help you greatly to fix it in your mind. In writing them, the basic rule is to write each letter from left to right, beginning with the small circle forming part of the main body of the letter–if there is such a small circle–and then trying to complete the letter in one stroke, unless the letter has two distinctive parts (such as "ญ YAW YEENG"). There are many simplifications used in writing Thai letters in everyday life, but the basic form does not change–the basic handwritten form is the same as the basic printed form. There are no capital letters used in Thai, though letters of a different size or style may be used for emphasis or clarity in some cases; nevertheless, no matter the size of the letter, it always has the same basic form.

2) As you can see, the simple Thai name for each consonant consists of the consonant sound itself plus an "AW" sound, giving us words that rhyme with "law, saw, etc." For most Thai consonants this simple "AW" name is enough. However, in some cases there are two or more consonants used for the same sound, making it necessary to distinguish between such consonants. To make such distinctions, the full name of the consonant may be used. This full name is simply the "AW" name plus an example of a word that is spelled with the consonant concerned. For example, in this lesson we have "ญ–YAW YEENG", meaning "the 'Y' consonant used in the word YEENG. Actually, all Thai consonants have a full name—not officially but only for convenience in learning them in school; however, since these full names are designed mostly to interest and impress little children, we will not use them any more than necessary. Thai adults generally rarely find it necessary to refer to the full name of a consonant, but when they do they seem to prefer using full names that are more "mature" and "less childish" than the ones they learned in school. For example, most Thai school-children learn the letter "R" (ร) as RAW REUA", but many Thai adults prefer to identify this letter as "RAW RAHK-SAH".

3) Some Thai consonants regularly have a different sound when used at the end of a syllable. For example, "ญ YAW YEENG" has a "Y" sound at the beginning of a syllable but an "N" sound at the end of a syllable. However, do not worry about this point at this time.

EXERCISES

Introduction. The exercises in each lesson are designed to review the new points made in each lesson, as well as points already learned in previous lessons. Try to do each exercise from memory, if possible. If necessary, consult the lesson itself or previous lessons, but try to do all the work yourself before checking your answers in the "Answer Key".

A) Write the English-phonetic names for the following Thai consonants.

1. ข	6. ง
2. ค	7. ญ
3. ช	8. ค
4. ง	9. ข
5. ญ	10. ช

B) Arrange these letters in Thai alphabetical order:

ข,   ง,   ญ,   ค,   ช

C) Write the Thai consonants that have the following numerical order in the Thai alphabet :–

11,   4,   13,   7,   10

D) Write the Thai letters for the following Thai consonants in English phonetics.

1. NGAW	6. KAW
2. SAW	7. YAW YEENG
3. CHAW	8. KAW
4. NGAW	9. CHAW
5. YAW YEENG	10. SAW

LESSON 2

THE MOST – IMPORTANT LOW – CLASS CONSONANTS (Continued)

(ท, ธ, น, พ, ฟ)

Table No. 2

Low–Class Consonant	Numerical order in Thai Alphabet	Name of the Consonant in English Phonetics	Equivalent Sound in English
ท	23	TAW TAH-HAHN	T
ธ	24	TAW TOHNG	T
น	25	NAW	N
พ	30	PAW PAHN	P
ฟ	31	FAW	F

EXERCISES

A) Write the English-phonetic names for the following Thai consonants.

1. น   6. พ   11. ป

2. ฟ   7. บ   12. ธ

3. ญ   8. ท   13. พ

4. น   9. ธ   14. ค

5. ฟ   10. ง   15. ท

B) Arrange these letters in Thai alphabetical order :–

ป, ธ, ฟ, น, ค, บ, ญ, ท, พ, ง.

C) Write the Thai consonants that have the following numerical order in the Thai alphabet :—

   30, 7, 25, 4, 24, 10, 23, 13, 31, 11

D) Write the Thai letters for the following Thai consonants in English phonetics

1. PAW PAHN   9. PAW PAHN
2. TAW TAH-HAHN   10. TAW TAH-HAHN
3. KAW   11. NGAW
4. FAW   12. TAW TOHNG
5. TAW TOHNG   13. NAW
6. NAW   14. CHAW
7. SAW   15. YAW YEENG
8. FAW

LESSON 3

THE MOST–IMPORTANT LOW–CLASS CONSONANTS (continued)

(ภ, ม, ย, ร, ล, ว, ฮ)

Table No. 3

Low–Class Consonant	Numerical order in Thai Alphabet	Name of the Consonant in English Phonetics	Equivalent Sound in English
ภ	32	PAW SAHM-PAO	P
ม	33	MAW	M
ย	34	YAW YAHK	Y
ร	35	RAW	R
ล	36	LAW	L
ว	37	WAW	W
ฮ	44	HAW	H

EXERCISES

A)   Write the English–phonetic names for the following Thai consonants.

1. ว	7. ฟ	13. ภ	19. ร
2. ภ	8. ฝ	14. ฉ	20. ฆ
3. ย	9. ม	15. ท	21. ณ
4. ล	10. ญ	16. ย	22. ป
5. ฮ	11. ส	17. ค	23. พ
6. ม	12. ว	18. ธ	24. ร

B)   Arrange these letters in Thai alphabetical order :—

1. ล, ค, ฟ, ญ, ง, ย, ม, ท

2. ฮ, ป, ว, ภ, ธ, ช, ร, น

3. ม, น, พ, ล, ช, ฟ, ง, ค

C)   Write the Thai consonants that have the following numerical order in the Thai alphabet.

1. 25, 31, 35, 44, 4, 10, 13, 33

2. 37, 11, 10, 7, 32, 36 30, 4

3. 23, 24, 34, 44, 31, 11, 13, 10

D)   Write the Thai letters for the following Thai consonants in English phonetics.

1. MAW	9. HAW	17. WAW
2. CHAW	10. KAW	18. NGAW
3. PAW SAHM-PAO	11. LAW	19. RAW
4. YAW YAHK	12. PAW SAHM-PAO	20. WAW
5. NGAW	13. FAW	21. NAW
6. TAW TOHNG	14. TAW TAH-HAHN	22. SAW
7. RAW	15. YAW YAHK	23. LAW
8. PAW PAHN	16. YAW YEENG	24. HAW

LESSON 4

REVIEW OF THE MOST–IMPORTANT
LOW–CLASS CONSONANTS

Note. Review tables such as the one in this lesson are meant to be used only as a handy reference for you, since they consolidate what has been convered in the preceding lessons. There are no exercises in this lesson.

Review Table No. 1

Low–Class Consonant	Numerical order in Thai Alphabet	Name of the Consonant in English Phonetics	Equivalent sound in English
ค	4	KAW	K
ง	7	NGAW	NG
ช	10	CHAW	CH
ซ	11	SAW	S
ญ	13	YAW YEENG	Y
ท	23	TAW TAH-HAHN	T
ธ	24	TAW TOHNG	T
น	25	NAW	N
พ	30	PAW PAHN	P
ฟ	31	FAW	F
ภ	32	PAW SAHM-PAO	P
ม	33	MAW	M
ย	34	YAW YAHK	Y
ร	35	RAW	R
ล	36	LAW	L
ว	37	WAW	W
ฮ	44	HAW	H

LESSON 5

VOWELS WRITTEN AFTER A CONSONANT

Introduction. As mentioned before, Thai consonants and Thai vowels are considered separately and are governed by different rules. The basic Thai alphabet consists only of 44 consonants; however, there are also 32 basic vowels, which are used with consonants to form words but which are not counted as part of the 44-letter Thai alphabet. There are several peculiar features about Thai vowels that you may find rather strange at first, but you will see that Thai vowels—the same as consonants—are orderly, consistent, and easy to read, once you learn the system.

Thai vowels are written in various positions with relationship to the consonants with which they are used. In this lesson we introduce you to the vowels that are written **after** the consonants with which they are used, since these vowels are in some ways the easiest ones to learn for those new to the peculiarities of the Thai language.

Don't worry about the meanings of the Thai words (we use some Thai words in this lesson as examples to show you simple word construction using consonants and vowels you have already learned). Vocabulary and grammar work will begin soon. These beginning lessons are very simply designed in order to get you somewhat accustomed to Thai letters before starting to concern yourself with meanings, translations, grammar, construction, etc.

Note. The same as with consonants, we also show the alphabetical order for vowels in order gradually to familiarize you with Thai-language dictionary word-order. However, bear in mind that vowels are not used alone in Thai; they are always used with at least one consonant; thus, Thai vowels depend on Thai consonants, while Thai consonants take alphabetical precedence over Thai vowels. Although there are technically 32 basic Thai vowels, there are only 26 separate dictionary distinctions in the alphabetical list of Thai vowels. This is because some of the 32 basic vowels actually are vowel substitutes formed through the use of consonants, Therefore, the numbers we give you to remember each vowel by refer to the numerical order a vowel has in the dictionary alphabetical list of 26 vowels, If you can remember these numbers, they will help you greatly when you start using a Thai dictionary. (We almost forgot to mention that some vowels are unwritten, but we are going to concern ourselves with the easy written ones first.)

* * * * *

Table No. 4
Vowels Written After a Consonant
(1)

า = AH, as in f<u>a</u>ther

A) **Numerical dictionary order:**— 4

B) **Examples :**—

   1. ม + า = มา (MAH)
   2. น + า = นา (NAH)
   3. ย + า = ยา (YAH)

C) **Remarks.** There is no distinctive name for each vowel in Thai, as there is for consonants. If one wishes to refer to a certain vowel, he simply says "SAH-RAH" plus the vowel sound itself. "SAH-RAH" means "vowel"; therefore, "SAH-RAH AH" means "the vowel า". (Technically, we should not write a vowel alone, since a vowel must always be used with a consonant. However, it is necessary to write vowels alone for the purpose of teaching them, as they do in Thai schools also.) Actually, nowadays few people take the trouble to say "SAH-RAH" when they refer to a vowel; they usually say only the vowel sound itself, as in English.

---

(2)

ะ = AH! (A brief emphatic "AH" sound; please note that we use an exclamation point to indicate this brief, emphatic sound that is peculiar to certain Thai vowels.)

A) **Numerical dictionary order :**– 1 (Please note that this vowel takes dictionary precedence over "า‑‑AH"; we have listed them out of sequence for the sake of facility in introducing them.)

B) **Examples :**–

    1. น + ะ = นะ (NAH!)

    2. ร + ะ = ระ (RAH!)

    3. ย + ะ = ยะ (YAH!)

C) **Remarks.** All Thai vowels have either a normal long sound, as with the vowel "า", or a brief, emphatic sound, as with the vowel "ะ". You will learn later on that the distinction between ordinary long vowels and brief emphatic vowels is important with regard to the tone rules. Actually, the words and syllables we introduce as examples in this lesson, do not all have the same tone. However, it is not worthwhile for you to concern yourself with these tonal distinctions at this time. You will be able to learn them easily enough later on, and they are not as difficult or as important as you may think.

(3)

°า = AH!M, as in French **"femme"** or as in American **"Tom"**.

A) **Numerical dictionary order :**-- 5

B) **Examples :**--

    1. น + °า = น̊า (NAH!M)

    2. ท + °า = ท̊า (TAH!M)

    3. ค + °า = ค̊า (KAH!M)

C) **Remarks.**

    a) As you can see, the vowel "°า" actually is made up of two parts and also contains a consonant sound (M) as well as a vowel sound (AH!). In the latter respect (containing both a vowel and a consonant sound), this vowel is different from most other Thai vowels. However, you will see later on that many Thai vowels are composed of more than one part, as "°า" is.

    b) Note that we again use an exclamation point to distinguish between this short-emphatic vowel sound ("°า--AH!M) and the combined vowel-consonant sound of "าม-- AHM", as in "นาม--NAHM". However, for speaking purposes you will find that the distinction between long vowels and brief-emphatic ones is not closely followed in normal everyday speech. Thus--except for certain words--you will still be understood even though you use a long vowel sound in place of a brief, emphatic one.

EXERCISES

A) Write the following Thai spellings in English phonetics.

1.	พาน	11.	ทำ
2.	ชาม	12.	ช่ำ
3.	ช่ำ	13.	ชะ
4.	นาน	14.	นาม
5.	ยาง	15.	คะ
6.	ระ	16.	นะ
7.	ลาง	17.	ฮา
8.	วา	18.	งาน
9.	ญาณ	19.	ธาน
10.	ฟาง	20.	ภำ

B) Write the Thai spelling for the following English phonetics.

1.	KAH!M	11.	NGAH
2.	RAH!	12.	MAH
3.	SAH!M	13.	CHAHNG
4.	NAHM	14.	MAHN
5.	PAHN (2 ways)	15.	NAH!M
·6.	TAHN (2 ways)	16.	TAH!M (2 ways)
7.	FAH!M	17.	FAHM
8.	LAH!	18.	WAHNG
9.	HAHN	19.	YAHN (2 ways)
10.	KAH!	20.	RAHNG

C) List the following syllables and words in Thai alphabetical order. Take the consonants one by one, according to the
alphabetical order you have already learned. Then list all words
beginning with a certain consonant, according to the alphabetical
sequence of vowels you have already learned, before going on to
the next consonant.

1. ละ, พาน, ทำ, ทาม, วาง, ยาง, นาน, ชำ

2. ฮา, คะ, คาน, คาม, นำ, นาม, นะ, ธาม

3. วา, งาน, งา, วาง, วาม, ญาน, ลาม, ลาน

LESSON 6

VOCABULARY PRACTICE

Introduction. With this lesson begins your study of real Thai words, their meanings, construction, and the rather–informal grammar rules concerning them. We use only words formed from the 17 low–class consonants and the 3 vowels you have already learned. The vocabulary is listed in Thai alphabetical order, according to the rules we have already explained.

Table No. 5

Vocabulary			
Number	Thai Word	Phonetic Pronunciation	Translation(s)
1	คำ (noun)	KAH!M	word
2	งาน (noun)	NGAHN	work
3	ชาม (noun)	CHAHM	bowl (for eating)
4	ทา (verb)	TAH	paint, rubon, spread, apply
5	ทำ (verb)	TAH!M	do, make
6	นะ (adv. or helping verb)	NAH!	please, okay? all right? etc.

Note. "นะ" is a polite word used very much in informal everyday conversation, usually after a verb or at the end of a sentence. It is used variously for persuasion, to express or ask for agreement, as merely a polite filler–word, etc.

7	นาน (adv.)	NAHN	a long time
8	นำ (verb)	NAH!M	lead
9	พระ (noun)	PRAH!	Buddhist priest or monk
10	ภาระ (noun)	PAH-RAH!	burden, heavy responsibility

Number	Thai Word	Phonetic Pronunciation	Translation(s)
11	มา (verb)	MAH	come
12	ยา (noun)	YAH	medicine
13	ยาง (noun)	YAHNG	rubber
14	วา (noun)	WAH	(a Thai linear measure equal to 2 meters)
15	วาง (verb)	WAHNG	put down, lay down
16	ฮา (interj)	HAH	(sound of laughter)

Notes.

1. We have not given you words beginning with all the low-class consonants you have learned because some of these consonants are used in relatively few words (some such words are often rather difficult in construction, and some of them are not used very much in ordinary everyday conversation). The words we have given you are ones we believe useful and worth learning in the initial stages of your study, but we have given you only enough to illustrate the various consonant-vowel constructions we have already learned. It won't be long now before you are using a Thai-English dictionary yourself, at which time you will be able rapidly to increase your vocabulary.

2. We have not mentioned this before, but perhaps we should point out that the only difficult Thai sound we have introduced you to so far is "ง——the 'NG' sound". Actually this sound is not difficult except when it comes at the beginning of a syllabl , as in the word "งาน——NGAHN" in this lesson. You will probably have to be content with learning to say an initial "NG" sound in this way from imitating speakers of Thai.

3. Most Thai verbs are very easy because there is only one form used for all persons, numbers, and tenses. You will see later on that everything can be made clear, however, by the context or

by the use of special helping words. The Thai language, we feel, can be made to express as precise a meaning as any other language can do, provided the writer of the Thai takes pains to do so. However, when there is no particular need to be precise, you will probably find that Thai seems to be rather liberal and easy in construction (thus compensating partially for some of the more-difficult things about the Thai language, such as the tones).

    4. Thai verbs are frequently used together to supplement one another－－for example: นำคนมา－－NAH!M KOH!N MAH = Bring the (a) person. (literally="lead the person come"). Thus, what actually happens is that two or more verbs are used together in certain cases to give a meaning that is expressed in English by one verb. In the example just mentioned, the two verbs "นำมา－－NAH!M MAH"="bring".

    5. The articles (a, an, the) are not necessary in Thai. Thus, in translating from Thai to English, you should use your imagination in order to arrive at the correct meaning. However, this does not mean that Thai is particularly inexact with regard to nouns; it is just that when there is no real reason for being precise, then Thai is not as precise as English is in regard to such matters. Nevertheless, the same as with verbs, the Thai language can be very precise in regard to nouns when it is necessary to do so.

    6. There is only one form for nouns in Thai. Singular and plural, and other distinctions, are taken care of－－when necessary－－by the use of helping or descriptive words of various kinds, as you will see later on.

    7. Note that we use a hyphen to connect syllables of the same word, as in "การะ－－PAH-RAH!".

    8. Basically the same parts-of-speech rules used in European languages, also govern Thai words. Thus, in a Thai dictionary the part of speech of a word is shown. There are a few minor differences, but it is not worthwhile to go into them at this time.

EXERCISES

Note. Please forgive us if our exercises seem boring or unnecessarily meaningless. You will no doubt appreciate the fact that we are simply trying to initiate you gradually into the mysteries of the Thai language and that it is difficult to concoct much meaning out of a limited number of words.

A) **Translate into English.** Remember to be liberal in your translations and to use your imagination in regard to such grammatical points as articles, tense, number of nouns, etc. Needless to say, our exercises at this stage usually do not constitute complete sentences, in good Thai. They are only a means to an end!

1. มาทำงาน

2. นำงานมา

3. วางยานะ

4. มาทำงานนาน

5. หายา

Note. We almost forgot to mention that Thai words are run together in normal writing, as they are in the preceding exercise. However, you should get used to this as soon as possible, and it is not really as confusing as you might at first think. You will see that there are convenient breaks in Thai writing—though not between every word, as in English—so that reading it is actually not difficult after one gets used to it.

B) **Translate into Thai.**
1. Ha! Ha! (Exclamation points are used in Thai also.)
2. Make a word.
3. the priest's bowl (We forgot to mention in the notes of this lesson that possession in Thai may be indicated simply by placing the possessed object before the possessor. There are other and more-precise ways, but this simple way is also acceptable.)

4. the burden of the work

5. Make some rubber.   ("Some", like articles, need not be translated in Thai.   However, you will see later on that there is a way to translate "some", just as there is a way to translate into Thai anything one can write or say in English.)

6. "wah", lead, please, word, bowl, burden

C) **Dictionary work.**   Arrange the following words into Thai dictionary order.   (We cannot resist giving you these dictionary exercises.   Realizing full well how time-consuming and frustrating they may be for you at first, we still feel they will be more than worth your while when you start using a Thai dictionary.   Take us, for example.   We learned Thai in many hard and wrong ways.   Thus, we still have trouble remembering the Thai alphabetical order, simply because we never learned it well to begin with.)

1. วา, นำ, ฮา, ภาระ, งาน, คำ

2. วาง, งาน, นาน, ช่าม, มา, ยา

3. นะ, ทา, ยาง, ภาระ, พระ, นาน

LESSON 7

VOWELS WRITTEN ABOVE A CONSONANT

Introduction. As already mentioned, Thai vowels are written in a variety of positions with relation to the consonant or consonants with which they are used. You have already learned the easiest vowels: those written **after** a consonant. The vowels in this lesson are the simple ones that are written **above** a consonant.

Table No. 6
Vowels Written Above a Consonant

(1)

◌ = IH!, as in h<u>i</u>t (Remember that our exclamation point indicates a brief, emphatic vowel sound as opposed to a normal, long vowel sound.)

A) **Numerical dictionary order :—** 6

B) **Examples :—**

 1. ย + ◌ + น = ยิน (YIH!N)

 2. ภ + ◌ + น = ภิน (PIH!N)

 3. ช + ◌ + น = ชิน (CHIH!N)

C) **Remarks.**

 1. Actually, this sound sometimes has a short, emphatic "EE" sound (EE!). However, you will see this for yourself later on.

 2. Please bear in mind that the meanings of the words or syllables we use in these introductory lessons on alphabet and reading are not important. In fact, some of them are meaningless. However, as we have already done previously, we will soon give you another lesson on vocabulary, incorporating the new letters you are now learning.

(2)

ꓼ = EE, as in me

  A) **Numerical dictionary order** :— 7

  B) **Examples** :—
    1. ม + ꓼ = มี (MEE)
    2. ช + ꓼ = ชี (CHEE)
    3. ม + ꓼ + นา = มีนา (MEE-NAH)

---

(3)

ꓽ = EU! (short EU)

  A) **Numerical dictionary order** :— 8

  B) **Examples** :—
    1. พ + ꓽ + ง = พึง (PEU!NG)
    2. ฟ + ꓽ + น = ฟึน (FEU!N)
    3. ท + ꓽ + ม = ทึม (TEU!M)

---

(4)

ึ = EU (no English equivalent – –must be learned by imitation)

A) **Numerical dictionary order :** – 9

B) **Examples :** –

1. ค + ึ + น = คึน (KEUN)

2. ช + ึ + น = ชึน (CHEUN)

3. ร + ึ + น = รึน (REUN)

C) **Remarks.**

1. Notice that all the vowels introduced in this lesson are based on a small quarter-moon shape. The vowel "ʌ– –IH!" is composed of this quarter-moon shape alone and is written with a single stroke. The other vowels in this lesson require at least two strokes (although in everyday handwriting little thought is given to the number of strokes – – some people can write almost anything in Thai, even a full word, with only one unbroken stroke! The fun comes when people such as us try to read it!)

2. Some people say that this vowel sound (ึ – –EU) resembles the French vowel sound in "coeur". However, we don't feel this approximation is very close. We feel a better comparison is with the slurred vowel sound in the English word "the", when it is spoken quickly. Even this comparison is not very accurate, though, so we fear there is no way out for you except to learn this sound by imitation. You will see that it is a distinctive sound in one way because the lips must be stretched sideways to some extent if the vowel sound is to be clearly and accurately produced.

EXERCISES

A)   Write the following Thai spellings in English phonetics.

1.	พี	11.	นิม
2.	ธิน	12.	ทิง
3.	ญูม	13.	ชี
4.	ชิน	14.	วิน
5.	คิน	15.	ภิง
6.	มี	16.	ยิน
7.	วิน	17.	ลิน
8.	วี	18.	ฮิ
9.	ธาน	19.	ญาน
10.	คะ	20.	พาน

B)   Write the Thai spellings for the following English phonetics.

1.	HEUN	11.	KEU!N
2.	WEE	12.	NGIH!
3.	LEE	13.	CHEUNG
4.	RIH!	14.	SIH!
5.	YEUNG (2 ways)	15.	TEU!NG (2 ways)
6.	MEE	16.	NEU!NG
7.	PEUNG (2 ways)	17.	FEUN
8.	TAH!M (2 ways)	18.	PAHN (2 ways)
9.	CHAHNG	19.	RAHNG
10.	FAH!M	20.	FAHM

C) **Dictionary work.** Put the following words and syllables into Thai alphabetical order.

1. นืม, ทึง, ชิ, วา, ช่ำ, ลาง

2. ฟาง, ภำ, งาน, ญิม, ชืน, คืน

3. ธาน, หำ, ช่ำ, คะ, วี, ริน

LESSON 8

REFERENCE LISTS UP–TO–DATE

Note. The lists in this lesson incorporate the main points that have been covered up to now. Since this lesson is intended only as a handy review and reference for you, no exercises are included in this lesson. Everything is listed in Thai alphabetical order.

Review Table No. 2
CONSONANTS

Nr.	Cons.	Dictionary order	Name in Phonetics	Equivalent sound	
				Initial	Final
1	ก	4	KAW	K	K
2	ง	7	NGAW	NG	NG
3	จ	10	CHAW	CH	T
4	ช	11	SAW	S	– –
5	ญ	13	YAW YEE!NG	Y	N
6	ฑ	23	TAW TAH!-HAHN	T	T
7	ต	24	TAW TOH!NG	T	T
8	น	25	NAW	N	N
9	พ	30	PAW PAH!N	P	P
10	ฟ	31	FAW	F	F(rare)
11	ภ	32	PAW SAH!M-PAO!	P	P
12	ม	33	MAW	M	M
13	ย	34	YAW YAH!K	Y	vowel
14	ร	35	RAW	R	N
15	ล	36	LAW	L	N
16	ว	37	WAW	W	vowel
17	ส	44	HAW	H	– –

Notes. 1) As you can see, we have slightly changed the phonetics in some cases, in order to be more phonetically exact, now that you understand our phonetic use of the exclamation point.

2) As mentioned before, certain consonants have one sound at the beginning of a syllable but a different one at the end of the syllable. We have shown you these different distinctions in the foregoing table. Technically, there are only eight terminal consonant sounds in the Thai language, but you will find exceptions. Notice that we have indicated that certain consonants are not used at the end of a syllable at all, while certain consonants actually have a vowel sound when used at the end of a syllable.

Review Table No. 3
Vowels

Nr.	Vowel	Dictionary order	Phonetics & Equiv. sound	Examples
1	–ะ	1	AH!	นะ, ระยะ (NAH!, RAH!-YAH!)
2	–า	4	AH	มา, รามา (MAH, RAH-MAH)
3	–ำ	5	AH!M	นำ, ทำ (NAH!M, TAH!M)
4	–	6	IH!	ยิน, ชิน (YIH!N, CHIH!N)
5	–	7	EE	มี, ชี (MEE, CHEE)
6	–	8	EU!	พึง (PEU!NG)
7	–	9	EU	คืน, ชืน (KEUN, CHEUN)

Review Table No. 4

Vocabulary

Number	Thai Word	Phonetics	Translation(s)
1	คำ (noun)	KAH!M	word
2	งาน (noun)	NGAHN	work
3	ชาม (noun)	CHAHM	bowl (for eating)
4	ทา (verb)	TAH	paint, rub on, spread on, apply
5	ทำ (verb)	TAH!M	do, make
6	นะ (adv. or helping verb)	NAH!	please, okay ? all right ?, etc.
7	นาน (adv.)	NAHN	a long time
8	นำ (verb)	NAH!M	lead
9	พระ (noun)	PRAH!	Buddhist priest or monk
10	ภาระ (noun)	PAH-RAH!	burden
11	มา (verb)	MAH	come
12	ยา (noun)	YAH	medicine
13	ยาง (noun)	YAHNG	rubber
14	วา (noun)	WAH	wah (a Thai measure = to 2 meters)
15	วาง (verb)	WAHNG	put down, lay down
16	ฮา (interj.)	HAH	ha (sound of laughter)

LESSON 9

ODDS AND ENDS UP-TO-DATE

Introduction. Before going on to some new letters of the Thai alphabet, let us introduce some of the miscellaneous peculiarities that can be demonstrated through the use of the consonants and vowels you have already learned.

I. Additional Vowel Sounds.

A) **The unwritten vowel sound of "OH!"** (brief, emphatic "OH", as in "home, bone, etc."). When two consonants are written together as one syllable, without any written vowels being present, the vowel sound of "OH!" is usually understood to connect these two consonants.

Examples.

1. คน = KOH!N

2. ลม = LOH!M

3. ทน = TOH!N

4. วง = WOH!NG

Remarks. Since such words as the foregoing do not contain any written vowels at all, they take complete alphabetical precedence over any words beginning with the same consonant used with a written vowel. For example, คน would be listed before คึน

B) **Consonants used as vowels.**

1. ไ + ย (at the end of a syllable) = AI (as in I, my, by); examples: นาย = NAI; ยาย = YAI

2. ไ + ว (at the end of a syllayble) = AO (as in how, now); examples: ชาว = CHAO; ลาว = LAO

II. Tones.

There are five tones in Thai (normal, rising falling, low, high), but there is no need to worry about tones yet.   For all practical purposes, all the syllables and words introduced up to now may be pronounced in a normal tone (not rising or falling, not high or low).   Actually, some of these words and syllables have a "high tone," but that is not very important at this time. Basically, most syllables formed with low-class consonants only (no high-class or middle-class consonants), have a normal tone (with the exceptions of some high-tone syllables, as already mentioned, and some falling tones).

III. Additional Vocabulary (in Thai alphabetical order)

Table No. 7

Number	Thai Word		Phonetics	Translations
1	คน	(noun)	KOH!N	person, people
2	คน	(verb)	KOH!N	stir (as a liquid)
3	ความ	(prefix)	KWAHM	(used as prefix with adjectives and adverbs to form abstract nouns)
4	ความงาม	(noun)	KWAHM-NGAHM	beauty
5	คำนำ	(noun)	KAH!M-NAH!M	foreword, preface
6	คืน	(noun)	KEUN	night
7	คืน	(verb)	KEUN	return something to someone, give back
8	งง	(adj.)	NGOH!NG	confused, perplexed
9	งา	(noun)	NGAH	ivory
10	งาม	(adj.)	NGAHM	beautiful

Number	Thai word	Phonetics	Translations
11	ชา (noun)	CHAH	tea
12	ชาญ (adj.)	CHAHN	expert, Chan (masculine first name)
13	ชาว (noun)	CHAO	inhabitant, native of a place (usually used before nouns)
14	ชาวนา (noun)	CHAO-NAH	rice farmer (inhabitant of a rice-farm)
15	ชาวลาว (noun)	CHAO-LAO	Laotian (native of Laos)
16	ชี (noun)	CHEE	Buddhist nun
17	ชิ (adverb or helping verb)	SEE !	(used for emphasis or orders after verbs or at end of sentence-see "Notes")
18	ทาง (noun)	TAHNG	way, route
19	ทำงาน (verb)	TAH!M-NGAHN	work, do work
20	ทำนา (verb)	TAH!M-NAH	farm, cultivate (rice)
21	ธง (noun)	TOH!NG	flag
22	นา (noun)	NAH	rice field, rice farm
23	นาง (noun)	NAHNG	woman, Mrs. (used mostly with the first name of married women)
24	นางนิภา (name)	NAHNG NIH!PAH	Mrs. Nipa
25	นาย (noun)	NAI	man, Mr., boss, master (used mostly with first names of men over 14, married or single)

Number	Thai Word	Phonetics	Translations
26	นายชาญ (name)	NAI CHAHN	Mr. Chan
27	นิภา (name)	NIH!-PAH	Nipa (feminine first name)
28	พา (verb)	PAH	lead someone
29	พามา (verb)	PAH MAH	bring someone
30	พิธี (noun)	PIH!TEE	ceremony
31	พึง (verb)	PEU!NG	should
32	ฟืน (noun)	FEUN	firewood
33	มี (verb)	MEE	have, has, there is, there are
34	ยืน (verb)	YEUN	stand, stand up
35	ระยะทาง (noun)	RAH!YAH!-TAHNG	distance (land measurement of the route)
36	ราคา (noun)	RAH-KAH	price, value
37	ลม (noun)	LOH!M	wind
38	ลา (verb)	LAH	to bid farewell to someone, to take leave of someone
39	ลาว (noun, adj.)	LAO	Laos, Laotian
40	ลืม (verb)	LEUM	forget
41	วิชา (noun)	WIH!-CHA	academic subject (also used as a masculine first name)
42	วิธี (noun)	WIH!-TEE	method, way of doing something

NOTES

Introduction. Well, still with us? If you have come this far and if you are able to do the exercises that follow these notes (at least the translating-into-English part), then you have gone a long way toward learning Thai. If you're having a great deal of trouble in recognizing letters and words, however, then perhaps you'd better review some of the earlier lessons before you go on. After this lesson we intend to move much faster. (Otherwise this little book will become larger than we had intended!)

1. Remember that possession in Thai may be shown simply by placing that which is possessed before the possessor.

Examples. ยาย่าใช YAH CHAHN (Chan's medicine)

ฟืนชาวนา FEUN CHAO—NAH (the farmer's firewood)

Later you will learn other ways to show possession; we are showing you only the easiest way here.

2. As in most other languages, there are also some words in Thai that have more than one meaning and/or are used as more than one part of speech, as in the case of "คน——KOH!N" (noun meaning "person" or verb meaning "stir"), in the vocabulary of this lesson.

3) The prefix "ความ——KWAHM" can be used with almost any adjective or adverb to form an abstract noun. Later on you will see that other prefixes are used to form other kinds of special words.

4) "คำนำ——KAH!M—NAH!M" is another example of a prefix being used to form another word. The word คำ is used as both a regular word (meaning "word") and as a prefix before many nouns, usually to indicate something in writing or in speaking.

5) "งาม——NGAHM" is the more-general term for "beautiful". There is another word you will learn later (สวย—SUAY, pronounced "sway", with a rising tone) that also means "beautiful" but which is used mostly for people.

6) Adjectives in Thai (with a few exceptions—especially numerical adjectives) always follow the noun they modify. In

Thai you may have a sentence without a verb; in cases where there is an adjective, the adjective may take the place of a "be" verb.   Thus, "Chan is confused." could be translated as ฉันงง --CHAHN NGOH!NG" (literally; "Chan confused").

7) The word "ชา--CHAH" really means "tea plant". Actually, a prefix for "water" should be used with ชา in order to say "tea น้ำชา–NAM–CHA" (liquid tea, that is.)   However, in ordinary speech simply the word ชา alone is often heard to mean "liquid tea".   This is an example of popular contractions in speech.

8) Don't forget our mentioning previously that certain consonants have one sound at the beginning of a syllable and another at the end of a syllable.   "ฉาญ--CHAHN" is an example of this peculiarity, and we hope you understand why.   (Because "ญ" has a "Y" sound at the beginning of a syllable but an "N" sound at the end of a syllable, as in ฉาญ.)

9) In the word "ซี--SEE!", please notice that the vowel sound of "อ" is not exactly "IH!", as is usually the case, but is more like "EE!".   As you will recall, we mentioned previously that "อ" does sometimes have an "EE!" sound instead of an "IH!" sound.

10) There are many words in this vocabulary that are simplifications of longer terms you will run into later on.   However, if you know such simplifications as these, then you will be better able to figure out the longer terms, maybe even without a dictionary.

11) As you probably know, first names are used in Thailand much more than last names.   The terms "นาย--NAI" and "นาง--NAHNG" may be used with first names only or with full names (but almost never with last names alone, as in western countries).

12) As in most languages, there are also often many ways in Thai to express more or less the same idea.   An example of this is "bring someone", which may be translated either as "พา มา--PAH MAH" or "นำมา--NAH!M MAH".   นำมา may

also be used to mean "bring something" (usually expressed, however, by เอามา–AO MA"), but พามา is rarely if ever used in this latter way.

13) As you may already know, Thailand is a country rich in "พิธี––PIH!–TEE". There must be hundreds or even thousands of various ceremonies in use or on the books, ranging from the informal family ceremonies to the very-formal royal or high-Buddhist ones.

14) The verb "ลา––LAH" usually implies making the traditional Buddhist "wai" expression of respect (placing the hands together under the chin), in addition to saying something polite, when taking leave of someone.

EXERCISES

Note. Admittedly we have given you a lot to remember and many new words to master in this lesson. However, we do not expect you to remember everything at this time. You will undoubtedly be unable to do the exercises from memory alone, but the practice and experience you gain in using the reference lists (consonants, vowels, vocabularies) will help you very much, we feel, in your desire to learn Thai. Basically, we are only trying to help you get over the humps and discouragement of the initial stages. After that you'll find it relatively easy to improve your Thai on your own, by using dictionaries, listening, observing, and speaking whenever you have the chance.

A) **Translate to English.** (Remember to use your imagination and make liberal translations when necessary. And let us re-emphasize that the following examples are certainly not "deathless Thai prose"; they are only contrived little thoughts to get you to put to work what you have learned.)

1. ชิมชา
2. นายชาญทำนา
3. นางนิภามีงางาม
4. พระทายา
5. นายชาญนำนางนิภามา
6. พังมีคำนำ
7. ชาวลาวลานายวิชา
8. มีคนคนชานาน
9. นายนำงามาคืน
10. ชาวนางง
11. พานายวิชามาชิ
12. ระยะทางมานานายชาญ
13. มีพระพานางนิภามาทำงาน
14. นายวิชามีธงงาม
15. มาทำพิธีนะ
16. ชาญลมนำพื้นมา
17. มีวธีทำนา
18. มีคนลาวมีภาระ
19. มาวางยางชิ
20. วา, ชาม, ฮา, ลม, ความงง, ราคา

B) **Translate into Thai.** (This exercise may of course be omitted if you are in a big hurry and want only to learn to read Thai. However, if you do have the time to practice writing Thai somewhat yourself, it will do wonders for you in helping you remember the words——unless you already have a photographic memory, of course!) Your translations may not agree exactly with ours, but you will be able to see whether you have put down the basic thoughts and have followed the few basic grammatical rules we have already mentioned.

1. There is a beautiful woman (who) has come.   (It is not necessary to translate "who", in this case.)

2. The Laotians work.

3. Bring Mrs. Nipa!

4. Stand up!

5. the distance to (coming to) Nai Wicha's rice-farm

6. The priest has some beautiful ivory.

7. Conduct the ceremony of returning the flag.

8. There is a method for forgetting the wind.

9. the price of Nai Chan's rubber

10. The rice-farmer brought Mr. Chan.

11. There is a nun standing.

12. The man brought the firewood.

13. night, stir, Mrs., should, wind, bid farewell

14. Laotian, method, word, wah, ha!, priest

15. a long time, please, bowl, burden, rubber, put down

16. confusion, beauty, tea, nun, distance, academic subject

C) **Arrange the following words into alphabetical (dictionary) order.**

1. วิธี, มี, ยืน, ท้า, คำ, ยา, ยาง, พระะ, ช่าม, สม, ลาว, พืน, ระยะทาง, นิภา, ราคา

2. ลา, งาน, ภาระ, นาน, วาง, พา, พิธี, สม, พง, ส่า, วา, น้ำ, นะ, ฮา, ท่า, นา

3. พืน, พง, พิธี, พามา, พา, พระะ, ภาระ, นาง, นาย, นายวิชา, นางนิภา, นายชาญ

LESSON 10

THE REMAINDER OF THE SIMPLE
ONE LOCATION VOWELS

Introduction. As promised in the preceding lesson, we are now going to start moving more rapidly, but if you have come this far with a reasonably good understanding of what has been covered up to now, then you should have no trouble. Don't think you have to memorize everything as it is introduced. The best way to learn Thai——or any other language——is to understand the rules and then put them into practice as much as possible until they become, in effect, memorized as a matter of course, while at the same time knowing how to clear up one's doubts by oneself, through the use of reference material.

The vowels we have already given you are those written after a consonant and above a consonant. Now we will give you all the one-location vowels in the following table, plus the vowel substitutes and unwritten vowels that we have already covered or that can be covered on the basis of the consonants you already know. By "one–location" vowels, we mean vowels that are written only in one place (after, above, before, or under a consonant). Later on you will see that a few vowels are composed of more than one part, written in more than one location.

＊ ＊ ＊ ＊ ＊

Table No. 8

One--Location Vowels (Including Those Already Introduced)				
Nr.	Vowel	Dictionary order	Written Location	Phonetics	Example & REMARKS
1	ะ	1	after	AH!	อะ——LAH! ——
2	ั	2	above & between	AH!	มัน——MAH!N; called— "MAI-HAN-AGAT"
3	า	4	after	AH	อา——LAH ——
4	ํา	5	after	AH!M	นํา——NAH!M; actually this vowel is written in two parts but is considered as a one-location vowel
5	ิ	6	above	IH!	ทิน——TIH!N; sometimes has sound of "EE!"
6	ี	7	above	EE	มี——MEE ——
7	ึ	8	above	EU!	พึง——PEU!NG ——
8	ื	9	above	EU	คืน——KEUN ——
9	ุ	10	under	OO!	ทุน——TOO!N; like vowel sound in "boot"
10	ู	11	under	OO	คูณ——Koon ——
11	เ	12	before	EH	เช่น——CHEHN; like vowel sound in "get"
12	แ	21	before	AA	แทน——TAAN; like vowel sound in "tan, man" (Amer. pronunc.)
13	โ	23	before	OH	โค——KOH ——
14	ใ	25	before	AI!	ใน——NAI!; called "MAIMUAN"
15	ไ	26	before	AI!	ไพ——PAI!; called "MAIMALAI"

Unwritten Vowels and Vowel Substitutes

1) OH! (between two consonants of the same syllable)
   Example :— คน KOH!N
2) AH! (after a single-consonant syllable preceding another syllable)
   Example :— ทนาย TAH!NAI
3) UA (somewhat like the vowel sound in "gruel")
   Formation :— by the use of the consonant "ว between two consonants.
   Example :— ควร——KUAN (remember that "ว" has the sound of "N" at the end of a syllable)
4) AO ("า" plus "ว" at the end of a syllable)
   Example :— ลาว——LAO
5) AI ("า" plus "ย" at the end of a syllable)
   Example :— นาย—— NAI

Table No. 9
Additional Vocabulary
(not in alphabetical order)

Thai	Phonetics	Translation(s)
1. ทนายความ	TAH!-NAI-KWAHM	lawyer, attorney
2. ทันเวลา	TAH!N WEH-LAH	on time
3. ทุน	TOO!N	capital, funds
4. ลำพูน	LAH!M-POON	Lampoon (town & province of Thailand)
5. เวลา	WEH-LAH	time
6. แทน (verb)	TAAN	substitute for, take the place of
7. โยน (verb)	YOHN	throw
8. ใน (prep.)	NAI!	in
9. ทำไม (adv.)	TAH!M-MAI!	why ?
10. ควร (verb)	KUAN	should

Note. ควร is used more than พึง.

EXERCISES

A) Translate into English.

1. ทนายความมีทุน

2. ในลำพูนมีชาวนา

3. นายชาญควรทำงานแทนนายวิชา

4. มาทันเวลานะ

5. โยน, ควร, ทำไม, แทน, ทนายความ, ทุน

B) Translate into Thai.
  1. The attorney should come.
  2. Mr. Chan threw the bowl.
  3. Mr. Wicha had time to work in place of ("in place of" = "substitute for") Mrs. Nipa.
  4. capital, Lampoon, on time, should, in, why

C) Arrange alphabetically.

1. ลำพูน, ทุน, ทนายความ, ทันเวลา, เวลา, แทน

2. ควร, คน, ทำไม, ใน, นาย, โยน, พระ, คำนำ

3. ทุน, ทาง, ระยะทาง, ทำนา, ทำงาน, งาน, พิธี

LESSON 11

THE REMAINDER OF THE LOW-CLASS CONSONANTS

Following is a complete list of all the 24 low-class consonants. The new ones introduced in this lesson are marked with a double asterisk in the left margin. (Use this list for reference only.)

Table No. 10
Low-Class Consonants

Nr.	Con-sonant	Dictionary order	Name in Phonetics	Equivalent Sound Initial	Final
1	ค	4	KAW KWAI	K	K
**2	ฅ	5	KAW KOH!N(obsolete)	— —	— —
**3	ฆ	6	KAW RAH!-KAH!NG (rare)	K	K
4	ง	7	NGAW	NG	NG
5	ช	10	CHAW CHAHNG	CH	T
6	ซ	11	SAW	S	T
**7	ฌ	12	CHAW CHUH (very rare)	CH	T
8	ญ	13	YAW YEE!NG	Y	N
**9	ฑ	17	TAW MOH!N–TOH (rare)	T	T
**10	ฒ	18	TAW POO–TAO! (rare)	T	T
**11	ณ	19	NAW NEHN	N	N
12	ท	23	TAW TAH!–HAHN	T	T
13	ธ	24	TAW TOH!NG	T	T
14	น	25	NAW NOO	N	N
15	พ	30	PAW PAH!N	P	P
16	ฟ	31	FAW	F	F
17	ภ	32	PAW SAH!M–PAO!	P	P
18	ม	33	MAW	M	M
19	ย	34	YAW YAH!K	Y	(vowel)
20	ร	35	RAW	R	N
21	ล	36	LAW LEE!NG	L	N
22	ว	37	WAW	W	(vowel)
**23	ฬ	42	LAW JOO!–LAH (rare)	L	N
24	ฮ	44	HAW	H	— —

NOTES

1) Note that consonant ||2 (ฅ) is obsolete; however, it is still considered as part of the 44–consonant Thai alphabet and may sometimes be found in older Thai-language books.

2) Note that we have given the full names for a great many consonants in this list, in order to distinguish clearly between those that have the same sound.   Let us re-emphasize that these full-consonant names are only for convenience in identification. They are used very little in real-life Thai conversation among adults.

3) You may wonder why there are so many consonants in Thai that duplicate the sounds of other consonants. The main reason is that Thai has borrowed heavily from the Sanskrit and Pali languages in the past, and it was desired to retain distinctive letters that would indicate the etymology of certain words. In addition, when the Thai language began to be written, it was found necessary or desirable to add certain consonants for use in writing native Thai syllables and words.

4) Most of the seven new consonants introduced in this lesson are used very little; however, you should be able to recognize them since some of them are used in certain words that are frequently encountered.

5) Technically speaking, there are only 8 consonant sounds in Thai at the end of syllables, as previously mentioned.   That is why such consonants as "จ", "ญ", and "ล" have one sound at the beginning of a syllable and another at the end of it. These 8 consonant sounds at the end of a syllable are K, NG, T, N, P, M, Y, and W. However, the "Y" and "W" sounds are actually vowel sounds, thus leaving only 6 actual terminal consonant sounds.   There are some exceptions, of course, especially for foreign words written in Thai, as when "ฟ" is used for a terminal "F".

Table No. 11
Additional Vocabulary
(not necessarily in alphabetical order)

Thai	Phonetics	Translation(s)
1. ใคร	KRAI !	who ? whom ?
2. ระฆัง	RAH!-KAH!NG	bell (usually a large one, as at a Buddhist temple)
3. พัฒนา (verb)	PAH!T-TAH!-NAH	develop

(*Note* that this word appears to have only two syllables: "พัฒ—PAH!T" and "นา—NAH". However, it is a characteristic of Thai that a final consonant of a syllable is often used twice: first as the final consonant of a syllable and then as a separate connecting syllable in itself, with an understood vowel sound of "AH!". Thus we have three syllables in this word.)

4. มณฑล (noun)	MOH!N-TOH!N	region, area (used nowadays mostly for military regions)
5. ภาค (noun)	PAHK	region (There used to be 9 ภาค in Thailand, each one consisting of many provinces.)

(*Note.* Now obsolete, from a national administrative standpoint.)

6. เณร (noun)	NEHN	Buddhist novice (usually younger than a priest or monk)

Thai	Phonetics	Translation(s)
7. คุณ (pron.)	KOO!N	you (also used politely with first names of people, either speaking with them or about them)
8. ควาย (noun)	KWAI	water buffalo
9. คนงาน (noun)	KOH!N-NGHAN	worker
10. ชนะ (verb)	CHAH!-NAH !	win, defeat (also used as masculine first name)
11. ชม (verb)	CHOH!M	praise, admire, look at
12. คำชม (noun)	KAH!M-CHOH!M	compliment, praise
13. ชวน (verb)	CHUAN	invite someone to do something
14. นม (noun)	NOH!M	milk, breast
15. นครพนม (noun)	NAH!-KAWN PAH!-NOH!M	Nakorn Panom (town and province in Northeastern Thailand)

(*Note.* The second syllable of นคร technically should be pronounced "KAWN"—not "KOR!N"; however, in reality it sounds more like "KORN", with a slight "r" sound.)

16. นคร	NAH!-KAWN	city, town

EXERCISES

A) Translate to English.

1. คุณชาญมีนาในนครพนม

2. มีคนนำระฆังมา

3. มีคนงานมาพัฒนาภาค

4. ชาวนาชวนคุณวิชามาชมควาย

5. มณฑล, ชนะ, คำชม, มด, นคร, ใคร

B) Translate to Thai.
1. Kuhn Chan, come to Nakorn Panom!
2. A worker admired the buffalo.
3. There are (Buddhist) novices, priests, nuns. (Note. Commas are used in Thai also, though not as much as in English.)
4. The lawyer defeats you.
5. Ask Mrs. Nipa to come to Nakorn Panom, please.
6. military region, region (containing many provinces), compliment (noun), city, bell, who

C) Arrange in alphabetical order.

1. ระฆัง, มณฑล, ชนะ, คนงาน, นม, นคร

2. นครพนม, เณร, คุณ, ภาค, ชม, ชวน

3. ควาย, คำชม, พระ, คุณ, ชี, ใคร

LESSON 12

THE 9 MIDDLE–CLASS CONSONANTS

Introduction. Now that we have covered all the 24 low-class consonants, let us go on to the middle-class consonants, which number only 9, in order that we may show you some useful words that employ these middle-class consonants. This will now give you 33 consonants out of the total of 44 consonants in the Thai alphabet. In the interest of a constant review and for your facility in doing the exercises, all these 33 consonants are hereinafter listed, with the new middle-class consonants being marked in the left margin with a double asterisk. (When you start learning about tones, you will then understand the importance of these "class" distinctions in consonants.)

Table No. 12
THE 33 LOW–CLASS AND MIDDLE–CLASS CONSONANTS

Dictionary order	Con-sonant	Type of Class	Name in Phonetics	Equiv. sound Initial	Final
** 1	ก	middle	GAW	G	K
4	ค	low	KAW KWAI	K	K
5	ฅ	low	KAW KOH!N	––	––
6	ฆ	low	KAW RAH!-KAH!NG	K	K
7	ง	low	NGAW	NG	NG
** 8	จ	middle	JAW	J	T
10	ช	low	CHAW CHAHNG	CH	T
11	ซ	low	SAW	S	T
12	ฌ	low	CHAW CHUH	CH	T
13	ญ	low	YAW YEE!NG	Y	N
**14	ฎ	middle	DAW CHAH!-DAH (see "Notes")	D	T

Dictionary order	Consonant	Type of Class	Name in Phonetics	Equiv. Sound	
				Initial	Final
**15	ฏ	middle	DTAW BPAH!-DTAH!K (see "Notes")	DT	T
17	ฑ	low	TAW MOH!N-TOH	T	T
18	ฒ	low	TAW POO-TAO!	T	T
19	ณ	low	NAW NEHN	N	N
**20	ด	middle	DAW DEH!K	D	T
**21	ต	middle	DTAW DTAO! (see "Notes")	DT	T
23	ถ	low	TAW TAH!-HAHN	T	T
24	ธ	low	TAW TOH!NG	T	T
25	น	low	NAW NOO	N	N
**26	บ	middle	BAW	B	P
**27	ป	middle	BPAW (see "Notes")	BP	P
30	พ	low	PAW PAH!N	P	P
31	ฟ	low	FAW	F	F
32	ภ	low	PAW SAH!M-PAO!	P	P
33	ม	low	MAW	M	M
34	ย	low	YAW YAH!K	Y	(vowel)
35	ร	low	RAW REUA	R	N
36	ล	low	LAW LEE!NG	L	N
37	ว	low	WAW	W	(vowel)
42	ฬ	low	LAW JOO!-LAH	L	N
**43	อ	middle	AW (see "Notes")	AW	AW
44	ฮ	low	HAW	H	--

NOTES

1) The sound of "ก" at the beginning of a syllable is represented by most Thai people in English as "K", while the real Thai "K" sounds are represented by them as "KH". Please remember, however, that the Thai "ก" is always a hard "G" (as in "give") and never a soft "G" (as in "general"). Actually, we would prefer also to use a phonetic "K" in this book for "ก" (G), as we feel it is best for our readers to get used to the prevailing centuries-old phonetic preferences for Thai-to-English transliteration. (Probably 99% of the Thais do use "K" for "ก", and indeed this is now the official Thai-government transliteration for "ก". However, we know from experience how hard it is to get used to pronouncing a "K" as a "G", so we try to help you over the initial "strangeness" of Thai by using a "G" for "ก".

2) The sound of "จ" at the beginning of a syllable is represented by many Thai people in English as "CH", while the real Thai "CH" sounds are represented by them as "CH" also, or perhaps even as "J". Needless to say, there is widespread disagreement and confusion about transliterating Thai into Roman letters, and you have probably encountered some of this confusion or disagreement yourself. (We once had the honor of receiving a letter from H.R.H. Prince Wan Waithyakorn, who stated that he had to spend five busy years of his life before he could get the Royal Institute to promulgate a phonetic system of transcription, with one end result being that a certain street that used to be known as "Soi Drabya" is now "Soi Sap".) (It should be noted that the official transliteration for "จ" should be "CH", but this is one case where we feel there is simply no valid reason for official refusal to distinguish between "จ" and the "CH" sounds in phonetics. We therefore insist on using "J" for "จ".)

3) Two of these middle-class consonants (ฎ and ฏ) are not used very much, but the other 7 are very important.

4) The sound of "DT" (in ต and ฏ) is only our phonetic way of expressing this Thai sound, which is a mixture of a "D" and a "T" and has rather an explosive sound. It must be learned by imitation. (The official phonetic symbol for this sound is "T", while the real "T" sounds are "TH".)

5) The sound of "BP" (as in ป) is also only a phonetic convenience for us. This sound is a cross between a "B" and a "P" and also has a rather explosive sound. (If you know Chinese, then the sounds of ต and ป will of course be easy for you, since both these sounds are used in Chinese also.) The official symbol for this sound is "P", the real "P" sounds are "PH".

6) We have added a full name for ร (RAW REUA), since in real life it is sometimes necessary to distinguish clearly between ร and ล, due to the fact that these two consonants are often transposed, both in speaking and writing. (That is one reason why you will sometimes see Thai people spelling an English name or word with an "R" instead of an "L", both in English and in Thai phonetics. (Thai phonetics for an English language word : "THAP SAP – ทับศัพท์ ". They have been made so conscious of the fact, by various sources, that they should not use an "L" in place of an "R" –– it sounds too Chinese? – that they sometimes overdo it. On the radio, for example, one can hear announcers who pronounce almost all their "L s" as "R s".)

7) The middle-class consonant อ is perhaps the most useful but also the most peculiar consonant in Thai. It is used both as a consonant and a vowel, is often silent, and technically is used as a silent consonant with vowels whenever it is necessary to show only a vowel sound. (You may remember our stating earlier that Thai vowels technically should not be written without an accompanying consonant. The proper way, using อ as a silent consonant, is thus :– อา = AH; อี = EE; อะ = AH!; etc.)

8) In Lesson 15 we will introduce you to the tonal system in Thai. (But right now you have many new letters to fix in your mind. No?)

Table No. 13

Additional Vocabulary

(not necessarily in alphabetical order)

1. มาก	MAHK	very, much, many
2. กรุณา	GAH!-ROO!-NAH	please, kindly
3. กลับ	GLAH!P	return, come back, go back
4. กลับมา	GLAH!P MAH	come back
5. กลับไป	GLAH!P BPAI!	go back
6. ไป	BPAI!	go
7. กับ	GAH!P	with
8. การ	GAHN	(prefix used before verbs to form gerunds)
9. ไกล	GLAI!	far, far away
10. จะ	JAH!	shall, will
11. ใจ	JAI!	heart, soul, mind (a vague term)
12. ดี	DEE	good
13. ใจดี	JAI!-DEE	good-hearted, with a good disposition
14. ดีใจ	DEE-JAI!	happy, pleased
15. กฎ	GOH!T	rule, regulation
16. กระทรวง	GRAH!-SUANG	ministry
(*Note.* "ทร" at the beginning of a syllable usually="S".)		

17.กฎกระทรวง	GOH!T GRAH!-SUANG	ministerial regulation
18. กบฏ	GAH!-BOH!T	rebel (noun)
19. ตัว	DTUA!	animal, insect
20. ตี	DTEE	whip, beat
21. บอก	BAWK	say, tell
22. บางที	BAHNG-TEE	perhaps, maybe
23. บาท	BAHT	baht (Thai currency)
24. ปรานี (often written ปราณี)	BPRAH-NEE	Prani (feminine first name)
25. ความประนี	KHWAHM-BPRAH-NEE	mercy
26. อะไร	AH!-RAI!	what
27. แปด	BPAAT	eight

EXERCISES

Note. Since we are trying to move very quickly in this book now (and hoping you don't desert us), we are going to eliminate henceforward all exercises except the Thai-to-English translation work.   At this point we feel it is important for you to build up your working recognition-vocabulary as quickly as possible.   It is not necessary that you also be able to write every word and be able to use it in a sentence.   Those things will come later.

Translate into English

    1. กรุณากลับมากับคุณปราณี

    2. คุณจะไปกระทรวงอะไร ?

3. ราคาแปดบาท

4. คุณวิชาดีใจมาก

5. คนใจดีมีความปรานี

6. มีการพัฒนามาก

7. ไปบอกนางนิภา

8. บางทีคุณชาญจะไปไกล

9. ชาวนามีควายแปดตัว

10. มีคนกบฏกลับมาแปดคน

11. มีกฎกระทรวง

12. ชาวนาตีควายนาน

13. ใครจะไปนครพนม?

14. ไปบอกคนงาน

15. คุณชนะชมคุณปรานี

Notes. 1. Notice that adjectives usually come after the noun they modify. In sentence 2 above, "อะไร" is an interrogative adjective.

2. However, numerical adjectives usually come **before** the noun they modify, as in sentence # 3 above.

3. Remember to make liberal translations. The important thing is to have the same meaning. There may be better ways to express some of the above meanings iu Thai, but these are only simple sentences for practice.

4. In sentences ⫢ 9 and ⫢ 10, notice that we say "buffaloes, eight animals" and "rebels, eight persons". These are examples of the classifying nouns "ตัว" and "คน" used with numbers. You will see later on that nouns in Thai are classified under a certain "classifying noun", and these classifying nouns are used with the ordinary nouns in some cases. (Don't try to understand the logic of this matter at this time; just be able to recognize and understand it.)

LESSON 13

THE HIGH–CLASS CONSONANTS

Note. This lesson completes the 44-consonant Thai alphabet. The new consonants introduced in this lesson are the 11 "high-class consonants" and are indicated by double asterisks at the left of the Thai alphabetical order for the consonants. Notice that the names for the high-class consonants are spoken with a RISING TONE, indicated in phonetics by a small "r" in parentheses before a syllable with a rising tone. The RISING TONE is very easy to make: simply start the syllable in a rather low tone of voice and end it in a rather high tone.

Table No. 14
THAI CONSONANTS (Complete List)

Dictionary order	Con- sonant	Type of Class	Name in Phonetics	Equiv. Sound Initial	Final
1	ก	middle	GAW	G	K
** 2	ข	high	(r) KAW KAI!	K	K
** 3	ฃ	high	(r) KAW KUAT	K (obsolete)	K
4	ค	low	KAW KWAI	K	K
5	ฅ	low	KAW KOH!N	K (obsolete)	K
6	ฆ	low	KAW RAH!-KAH!NG	K	K
7	ง	low	NGAW	NG	NG
8	จ	middle	JAW	J	T
** 9	ฉ	high	(r) CHAW	CH	T
10	ช	low	CHAW CHAHNG	CH	T

Dictionary order	Consonant	Type of Class	Name in Phonetics	Equiv. Sound Initial	Final
11	ซ	low	SAW	S	T
12	ฌ	low	CHAW CHUH	CH	T
13	ญ	low	YAW YEE!NG	Y	N
14	ฎ	middle	DAW CHAH!-DAH	D	T
15	ฏ	middle	DTAW BPAH!-DTAH!K	DT	T
** 16	ฐ	high	(r)TAW (r)TAHN	T	T
17	ฑ	low	TAW MOH!N-TOH	T	T
18	ฒ	low	TAW POO-TAO!	T	T
19	ณ	low	NAW NEHN	N	N
20	ด	middle	DAW DEH!K	D	T
21	ต	middle	DTAW DTAO!	DT	T
** 22	ถ	high	(r)TAW (r)TOO!NG	T	T
23	ท	low	TAW TAH!-HAHN	T	T
24	ธ	low	TAW TOH!NG	T	T
25	น	low	NAW NOO	N	N
26	บ	middle	BAW	B	P
27	ป	middle	BPAW	BP	P
** 28	ผ	high	(r)PAW	P	P
** 29	ฝ	high	(r)FAW	F	——
30	พ	low	PAW PAH!N	P	P
31	ฟ	low	FAW	F	F
32	ภ	low	PAW SAH!M-PAO!	P	P
33	ม	low	MAW	M	M

Dictionary order	Con-sonant	Type of Class	Name in Phonetics	Equiv. sound	
				Initial	Final
34	ย	low	YAW YAH!K	Y	(vowel)
35	ร	low	RAW REUA	R	N
36	ล	low	LAW LEE!NG	L	N
37	ว	low	WAW	W	(vowel)
** 38	ศ	high	(r)SAW (r)SAH-LAH	S	T
** 39	ษ	high	(r)SAW REU-(r)SEE	S	T
** 40	ส	high	(r)SAW (r)SEUA	S	T
** 41	ห	high	(r)HAW	H	--
42	ฬ	low	LAW JOO!-LAH	L	N
43	อ	middle	AW	AW	AW
44	ฮ	low	HAH	H	--

Notes. 1) Note that there are three high-class "S" consonants. However, the most-common one is "ส"

2) The high-class "H" consonant "ห" is often silent, as you will see when get you into tones.

Table No. 15

Additional Vocabulary

(not necessarily in alphabetical order)

1.	ของ	(r)KAWNG	of, belonging to
2.	ฉัน	(r)CHAH!N	I, me (used mostly by women but may be used by anyone)
3.	รัฐบาล	RAH!T-TAH!-BAHN	government
4.	ถนน	TAH!-NOH!N	road, street, highway, avenue

5.	ถนนสีลม	TAH!-NOH!N (r)SEE-LOH!M	Silom Road (a street in Bangkok)
6.	ผม	(r)POH!M	I, me (used by males)
7.	ฝัน	(r)FAH!N	dream (verb)
8.	ประเทศ	BPRAH!-TEHT	country
9.	ประเทศไทย	BPRAH!-TEHT TAI!	Thailand (country of Thailand)
10.	ภาษี	PAH-(r)SEE	taxes
11.	สาม	(r)SAHM	three
12.	สอง	(r)SAWNG	two
13.	หก	HOH!K	six
14.	สิบ	SEE!P	ten
15.	หา	(r)HAH	look for, see someone (for a reason)
16.	ไหน (silent "H")	(r)NAI!	where (interrogative)
17.	ไหม	(r)MAI!	(helping word used at the end of a sentence to indicate a question)
18.	หรือ (silent ห and silent อ)	(r)REU	(helping word used at the end of a sentence to indicate a question)

Notes. 1) As mentioned before, it is not necessary to use a word between that possessed and the possessor in order to show possession. However, a clearer and more-common way to indicate possession is through the use of "ของ". For example : ประเทศของฉัน = my country.

2) There are many personal pronouns in Thai, varying with the circumstances. However, most of the time most women say "ฉัน" for "I", while men usually say "ผม".

3) Note that "รัฐบาล" seems to have only two syllables but really has three; the consonant "ฐ" is used as the final consonant of the first syllable and also as the second syllable in itself, with an understood "AH!" vowel sound.

4) Note that the consonant "ถ" in "ถนน" gives the second syllable a rising tone. Don't worry about such fine points for the time being, however.

5) The name of a country is usually prefaced by the word **ประเทศ** (country), as in **ประเทศสหรัฐอเมริกา** (BPRAH!–TEHT SAH!–HAH!–RAH!T AH!–MEH–RIH!–GAH, the United States of America).

6) The verb **หา** is used very much: "to see a doctor", "to see someone on business", "to see a friend", etc.

7) The best and about the only practical way to learn whether to use **ไหม** or **หรือ** at the end of a question is through observation, experience, and practice.

EXERCISES

Translate to English.

1. ฉันจะกลับไปประเทศของฉัน
2. คุณชาญทำงานกับรัฐบาลไทย
3. ผมจะไปถนนสีลม
4. ฉันผันดีมาก
5. ภาษีสิบบาท

6. ไปหาคุณนิภากับผมนะ

7. คุณจะไปไหน ?

8. คุณมีสามบาทไหม ?

9. ควายหกตัวหรือ ?

10. มีชายสองคนมาหาคุณ

———————

LESSON 14

A COMPLETE VOWEL LIST

Note. You have already been introduced to many vowels. This lesson will just about wind up our work on introducing vowels to you, except for a few details that may turn up later on. The vowels we have saved until now are those that consist of two or more parts, each of which is written in a different location. Following is a list of the 26 distinctive written vowels, listed according to alphabetical dictionary order. New vowels in this lesson are marked with a double asterisk on the left-hand side.

Table No. 12
The 26 Main Thai Vowels

Dict. order	Vowel	Written Location	Phonetics	Example		REMARKS
1	ะ	after	AH!	จะ	——JAH!	——
2	ั	above & between	AH!	กัน	——GAH!N	——
** 3	ัะ	combination	UA!	ผัวะ	——PUA!	very rare
4	า	after	AH	นา	——NAH	——
5	ํา	comb.	AH!M	นำ	——NAH!M	——
6	ิ	above	IH! or EE!	กิน	——GIH!N	——
				ดิน	——DEE!N	——
7	ี	above	EE	มี	——MEE	——
8	ึ	above	EU!	พึง	——PEU!NG	——
9	ื	above	EU	ลืม	——LEUM	——
10	ุ	under	OO!	คุณ	——KOO!N	——
11	ู	under	OO	คูณ	——KOON	——

Dict. order	Vowel	Written Location	Phonetics	Example	REMARKS
12	เ	before	EH	เวลา --WEH-LAH	--
** 13	เ-ะ	comb.	EH!	เตะ --DTEH!	--
** 14	เ-า	comb.	AO!	เขา --(r)KHAO!	--
** 15	เ-าะ	comb.	AW!	เกาะ --GAW!	--
** 16	เ- ̂	comb.	UH(as in "butter")	เดิน --DUHN	--
** 17	เ- ̀ย	comb.	IA	เสีย --SIA	--
** 18	เ- ̀ยะ	comb.	IA!	เหียะ--PIA!	very rare
** 19	เ- ̀อ	comb.	EUA	เสือ --(r)SEUA	--
** 20	เ- ̀อะ	comb.	EUA!	เกอะ --GEUA!	very rare
21	แ	before	AA	แปด --BPAAT	--
22	แ-ะ	comb.	AA!	แพะ --PAA!	rare
23	โ	before	OH	โกน --GOHN	--
** 24	โ-ะ	comb.	OH!	โปะ --POH!	rare
' 25	ใ	before	AI!	ใน --NAI!	used in only 20 common words
26	ไ	before	AI!	ไหม --(r)MAI	--

Unwritten Vowels & Vowel Substitutes

1) **OH!** (between two consonants of the same syllable)
   Example:- คน KOH!N

2) **AH!** (after a single-consonant syllable preceding another syllable)
   Example:- ทนาย TAH!–NAI

3) **AH! (two "ร" used together)
   Example:- สรรยา PAH!N–RAH!–YAH (The second ร is used twice: first as the final "N" sound of the first syllable and second as a separate "AH!" syllable in itself.)

4)   **AW (the final ร of a syllable, in some words)
     Example :– ศร (r)SAWN
5)   **AW (with an initial บ or ท, in some words)
     Example :– บรัษัท BAW–RIH!–SAH!T
                 ทรมาน TAW–RAH!–MAHN
  6)   **UA** (somewhat like the vowel sound in "gruel"; formed
by ว between two consonants)
     Example :– ควร ––KUAN
  7)   **AO** (า plus ว at the end of a syllable)
     Example :– ลาว ––LAO
  8)   **AI** (า plus ย at the end of a syllable)
     Example :– นาย ––NAI
9)   **UH (เ plus อ plus ะ)
     Example :– เลอะ ––LUH!
10)   **UH (เ plus อ)
     Example :– เรอ ––RUH
**11)   REU!, RIH!, or RUH (very rare; used mostly as RIH!)
     Formation :– by using the rare semi-consonant semi-
vowel ฤ.
     Example :– อังกฤษ AH!NG–GRIH!T

Table No. 17

Additional Vocabulary
(not necessarily in alphabetical order)

เตะ (verb)	DTEH!	kick
เขา	(r)KAO!	he, him, she, her
เกาะ	GAW!	island
เดิน (verb)	DUHN	walk
เสีย (verb)	(r)SIA	pay, pay out, lose
เสือ	(r)SEUA	tiger
ภรรยา	PAH!N–RAH!–YAH	wife

ศรแดง	(r)SAWN–DAANG (DAANG = red)	The Red Arrow (a popular Thai restaurant in Bangkok)
บริษัท	BAW–RIH!–SAH!T	company, firm (commercial)
ทรมาน (verb)	TAW–RAH!–MAHN	torture
เลอะ	LUH!	dirty, soiled
เรอ (verb)	RUH	belch
อังกฤษ (adj.)	AH!NG–GRIH!T	English
ภาษาอังกฤษ	PAH–(r)SAH AH!NG–GRIH!T	the English language, English

EXERCISES

Translate to English.

1. คุณวิชาเตะเขาหรือ ?
2. ประเหคไทยมีเกาะมาก
3. มีเสือเดินมาหาคุณ
4. ฉันเสียใจมาก
5. คุณชนะมีภรรยา
6. ไปศรแดงกันดีไหม ?
7. เขาทำงานบริษัทอะไร ?
8. เสือทรมานควาย
9. บางทีจะเลอะมาก
10. มีใครเรอ ?
11. ภาษาอังกฤษหรือภาษาไทย ?

LESSON 15

TONES AND TONE MARKS

Introduction. Well, we have held off on tones as long as we could, since they are usually the most discouraging thing for most foreigners learning Thai. However, be not dismayed (it says here!); tones are not all that difficult.

In all seriousness, Thai tone rules are very detailed and complicated, though they are orderly and well-organized. We do not propose at this time to show you all the Thai tone rules, however, but only to give you some examples of the most common tone rules in real Thai speech.

Technically speaking, each syllable in Thai has its own tone; therefore, you may have more than one tone in the same word. However, in actual practice, you will find that the most important tone is generally the one that is spoken clearly. Tones of secondary importance often "get lost".

There are five tones in Thai: normal, low, rising, falling, high. In our phonetics **we use nothing to indicate a normal tone** (spoken in a normal tone of voice, neither rising nor falling), **an "l" in parentheses to indicate a low tone** (spoken in a low tone of voice, neither rising nor falling), **an "r" to indicate a rising tone** (beginning low and going up), **an "f" to indicate a falling tone** (beginning high and coming down), and **an "h" to indicate a high tone** (spoken in a high, emphatic tone of voice, neither rising nor falling). If you are not accustomed to tones in speaking a language, then you will naturally find it difficult for a while, but one fine day you will find that tones seem natural to you and perhaps wonder how so many other languages have gotten along without them!

Although there are four written tone marks (to be covered later in this lesson), a written tone mark is not necessary for a syllable to have a certain tone. Other factors influencing the tone of a syllable (besides written tone marks) are the class of the initial and final consonants (low, middle, high) and the type of vowel sound (normal or short-emphatic).

If you don't already know the reason why tones are necessary in Thai, it is of course mainly because there are so many monosyllabic words with the same sound (to Western ears); the tones serve to distinguish clearly between the varying meanings of such words. In Thai, therefore, a tone is an integral part of a word, giving the word its unmistakable meaning (whether there is a written tone mark or not).

The four written tone marks in Thai are :—

1. " ' " MAI-EHK

2. " ʋ " MAI—TOH

3. " ᧡ " MAI-DTREE

4. " + " MAI-JATTAWA

Generally speaking, these tone marks are written above and on the right-hand side of the first consonant in a syllable (above a vowel, if a vowel is present above a consonant also.)

Now we will give you some vocabulary examples of the most important tone rules, and we hope this will whet your interest enough to go ahead and get into the finer points of tones in other more-detailed books on Thai. The best thing of all, however, is to practice trying to distinguish the important tones in spoken Thai and then trying to imitate them.

Vocabulary Examples of the Most - Important Tone Rules

1. **RISING TONE**

    A) **A high-class consonant plus a long vowel**

    Example : สี — —(r)SEE = color

    B) **A high-class consonant beginning a syllable that ends in a consonant sound of M, N, NG, W, or Y**

    Examples : สาม   — —(r)SAHM (= three)

    ทหาร   — —TAH!—(r)HAHN (= soldier)

    ฝัง   — —(r)FAH!NG (= bury)

    สาว   — —(r)SAO (= young woman)

    ไหน   — —(r)NAI! (= where ?——the "h" is silent)

C) Any syllable with **MAI–DTREE**

Examples: ตั๋ว ––(r)DTUA! (ticket, as a train ticket)

2. LOW TONE

A) **A high-class or middle-class consonant plus a short**
vowel

Examples: ถนน ––(l)TAH!–(r)NOH!N (= street)

จะ   ––(l)JAH! (shall, will)

B) **A syllable beginning with a high-class or middle-class**
consonant and ending in a consonant sound of K, P, or T.

Examples: หก   ––(l)HOH!K (= six)

แปด ––(l)BPAAT (= eight)

C) **A high-class consonant, plus a long vowel, plus a**
MAI-EHK tone mark

Example: สี่   ––(l)SEE (= four)

D) **A middle-class consonant plus a MAI-EHK tone mark**

Example: ก่อน––(l)GAWN (before)

3. FALLING TONE

A) **A high-class or middle-class consonant plus a MAI-TOH**
tone mark

Examples: ห้า   ––(f)HAH (= five)

บ้าน––(f)BAHN (= house)

B) **A low-class consonant plus a MAI-EHK tone mark**

Example: ท่าน––(f)TAHN (=you--polite and respectful
form)

C) **A syllable beginning with a low-class consonant, having**
a long vowel sound, and ending in a consonant sound of K, P, or T.

Examples: มาก ––(f)MAHK (= much, many, very)

ภาพ ––(f)PAHP (picture)

วาด ––(f)WAHT (= draw--verb)

4. HIGH TONE

   A) A low-class consonant plus a MAI-TOH tone mark

   Example :– ช้า – –(h)CHAH (slow, slowly)

   B) A syllable begining with a low-class consonant and ending in a short vowel sound

   Example :– นะ – –(h)NAH! (=please)

   C) A syllable beginning with a low-class consonant, having a short-emphatic vowel sound, and ending in a consonant sound of K, P, or T.

   Examples :– รัก – –(h)RAH!K (= love)

   นับ– –(h)NAH!P (count)

   พัดลม– –(h)PAH!T-LOH!M (= fan–noun)

5. NORMAL TONE

   A) A syllable beginning with a low-class consonant and ending with a low-class consonant with the sound of M, N, NG, W, or Y.

   Examples :– งาม – –NGAHM (= beautiful)

   ชาญ – –CHAHN (=Chan, masculine first name)

   ยัง – –YAH!NG (=yet, not yet, still)

   ลาว– –LAO (Lao, Laotian)

   นาย– –NAI (= Mr., master, boss)

   B) A syllable beginning with a middle-class consonant and ending with a low-class consonant with the sound of M, N, NG, W, or Y.

   Examples :– ดม – –DOH!M (sniff, smell of)

   การ– –GAHN (prefix used with verbs to form gerunds)

   บาง – –BAHNG (= thin)

   กาว – –GAO (= gum, glue)

   ตาย– –DTAI (= die)

C) A syllable beginning with a low-class or middle-class consonant and ending in a long vowel.

Examples :— นา — —NAH (=rice field)

ดี — —DEE (good)

EXERCISES

Note. Since this lesson is mostly for use as a not-too-detailed reference and inasmuch as many of the words used have already been introduced anyway, no exercise is felt necessary for this lesson.   It would be too confusing to have you try to give the correct tones for certain syllables or words, based merely on the admittedly sketchy outline we have given you in this lesson.

LESSON 16

ODDS AND ENDS

Introduction. In this final short lesson our objective is to point out to you some of the remaining important and useful things you should know in order to read and understand written Thai, as well as speak and understand spoken Thai. Since this lesson is intended primarily as a reference lesson for you, no exercises are felt necessary. By this time we sincerely hope you are making profitable use of Thai-English dictionaries.

Odds and Ends

1) The symbol "◌่" (MAI–DTAI!–KOO) is used to make a syllable have a short, emphatic vowel sound.

Example :– เป็น – –BPEH!N (=to be, is, are, etc.)

2) The symbol "◌์" (MAI–TAH!N–DTAH!–KAHT) is used to make one or more final consonants silent.

Examples :– อาจารย์ – –AH–JAHN (=teacher) (the ย is silent

พระจันทร์ – –PHRAH!–JAH!N (= moon)
(the final ท and ร are both silent)

3) The symbol " ๆ " (BPAI!–YAHN–NAWY) is used to abbreviate a long, well-known term; the symbol itself is not read.

Example :– กรุงเทพ ๆ ––GROO!NG TEHP (=Bangkok, the short name for the longer name)

ๆ พณ ๆ PHANA––TAHN (=His Excellency, Your Excellency)

4) The term "ๆลๆ" means "etc."; it is read as "ละ ––(h) LAH!".

5) The symdol " ๆ " (MAI–YAMOK) indicates that the preceding word is to be repeated; the symbol itself is not read.

Example :– ดี ๆ ––DEE DEE (=in a good way)

6) Most of the modern punctuation marks are used in Thai but not to a very great extent.

ANSWER KEY

** Lesson **1**

A) 1. SAW; 2. KAW; 3. CHAW; 4. NGAW; 5. YAW YEENG; 6. NGAW; 7. YAW YEENG; 8. KAW; 9. SAW; 10. CHAW.

B) ค, จ, ช, ช, ญ.

C) ช, ค, ญ, จ, ช.

D) 1. จ, 2. ช, 3. ช, 4. จ, 5. ญ, 6. ค, 7. ญ, 8. ค, 9. ช; 10. ช.

** Lesson **2**

A) 1. NAW; 2. FAW; 3. YAW YEENG; 4. NAW; 5. FAW; 6. PAW PAHN; 7. SAW; 8. TAW TAH–HAHN; 9. TAW TOHNG; 10. NGAW; 11. CHAW; 12. TAW TOHNG; 13. PAW PAHN; 14. KAW; 15. TAW TAH–HAHN.

B) ค, จ, ช, ช, ญ, ท, ธ, น, พ, ฟ.

C) พ, จ, น, ค, ธ, ช, ท, ญ, ฟ, ช.

D) 1. พ, 2. ท, 3. ค, 4. ฟ, 5. ธ, 6. น, 7. ช, 8. ฟ, 9. พ, 10. ท, 11. จ, 12. ธ, 13. น, 14. ช, 15. ญ.

**** Lesson 3**

A) 1. WAW;   2. PAW SAHM-PAO;   3. YAW YAHK;
4. LAW;   5. HAW;   6. MAW;   7. LAW;   8. FAW;   9. MAW;
10. YAW YEENG;   11. HAW;   12. WAW;   13. PAW SAHM-PAO;
14. NGAW;   15. TAW TAH-HAHN;   16. YAW YAHK;   17. KAW;
18. TAW TOHNG;   19. RAW;   20. NGAW;   21. NAW;   22. CHAW;
23. PAW PAHN;   24. RAW.

B) 1. ค, ง, ญ, ท, ฟ, ม, ย, ล.

2. ช, ซ, ธ, น, ภ, ร, ว, ฮ.

3. ค, ง, ซ, น, พ, ฟ, ม, ล.

C) 1. น, ฟ, ร, ฮ, ค, ช, ญ, ม.

2. ว, ช, ซ, ง, ภ, ล, พ, ค.

3. ท, ธ, ย, ฮ, ฟ, ซ, ญ, ช.

D) 1. ม, 2. ช, 3. ภ, 4. ย, 5. ง, 6. ธ, 7. ร, 8. พ,
9. ฮ, 10. ค, 11. ล, 12. ภ, 13. ฟ, 14. ท, 15. ย, 16. ญ,
17. ว, 18. ง, 19. ร, 20. ว, 21. น, 22. ช, 23. ล, 24. ฮ.

**** Lesson 5**

A) 1. PAHN;   2. CHAHM;   3. SAH!M;   4. NAHN;
5. YAHNG;   6. RAH!;   7. LAHNG;   8. WAH;   9. YAHN;
10. FAHNG;   11. TAH!M;   12. CHAH!M;   13. SAH!;   14. NAHM;
15. KAH!;   16. NAH!;   17. HAH;   18. NGAHN;   19. TAHN;
20. PAH!M.

B) 1. คำ   5. พาน, ภาน

2. ระ   6. ทาน, ธาน

3. ซำ   7. ฟา

4. นำ   8. ละ

9. ฮาน   15. นำ

10. คะ   16. ทำ, ธำ

11. งา   17. ฟ้าม

12. มา   18. วาง

13. ช้าง   19. ญาน, ยาน

14. มาน   20. ราง

C) 1. ช้ำ, ทาม, ทำ, นาน, พาน, ยาง, ละ, วาง.

     2. คะ, คาน, คาม, ธาม, นะ, นาม, นำ, ฮา.

     3. งา, งาน, ญาน, ลาน, ลาม, วา, วาง, วาม.

** **Lesson 6**

A) 1. Come to work.
2. Bring the work.
3. Lay the medicine down, please.
4. Come to work a long time.
5. Rub on the medicine.

B) 1. ฮา! ฮา!

     2. ทำคำ

     3. ชามพระ

     4. ภาระงาน

     5. ทำยาง

     6. วา, นำ, นะ, คำ, ชาม, ภาระ.

C) 1. คำ, งาน, นำ, ภาระ, วา, ฮา.

     2. งาน, ชาม, นาน, มา, ยา, วาง.

     3. ทา, นะ, นาน, พระ, ภาระ, ยาง.

** Lesson 7

A)
1. PEE	11. NEUM
2. TIH!N	12. TEU!NG
3. YIH!M	13. SEE!
4. CHEUN	14. NGIH!N
5. KEUN	15. PEUNG
6. MEE	16. YEUN
7. RIH!N	17. LIH!N (or LEE!N)
8. WEE	18. HEU
9. TAHN	19. YAHN
10. KAH!	20. PAHN

B)
1. ฮึน	11. คึน
2. วี๊	12. จิ๊
3. ลี๊	13. ชึง
4. ริ๊	14. ชิ๊
5. ญึง, ยึง	15. ทึง, ธิึง
6. มี๊	16. นึง
7. พึง, ภึง	17. พืน
8. ทำ, ธำ	18. พาน, ภาน
9. ชาง	19. ราง
10. ฟ้า	20. ฟาม

C)
1. ชำ, ชิ๊, ทึง, นืม, ลาง, วา.

2. คืน, งาน, ชืน, ญิม, ฟาง, ภำ.

3. คะ, ชำ, ทำ, ธาน, ริน, วี๊.

⁻* Lesson 9

A) 1. The nun has some tea.

2. Mr. Chan farms.

3. Mrs. Nipa has some beautiful ivory

4. Mr. Chan rubs on some medicine.

5. Mr. Chan has brought Mrs. Nipa.

6. It should have a foreword.

7. The Laotian took leave of Mr. Wicha.

8. Someone stirred the tea a long time.

9. The boss returned the ivory.

10. The Laotian is confused.

11. Bring Mr. Wicha!

12. the distance to (come to) Mr. Chan's rice farm,

13. (There was) a priest (who) brought Mrs. Nipa to (in order to) work (do work).

14. Mr. Wicha has a beautiful flag.

15. Come to do (participate in, perform) the ceremony, please.

16. Chan forgot to bring the firewood.

17. There is a method for rice-farming.

18. There are some Laotians who have burdens.

19. Come and put down the rubber!

20. "wa", bowl, ha, wind, confusion, price,

B) 1. มีนางงามมา

2. ชาวลาว (คนลาว) ทำงาน

3. พา (นำ) นางนิภามานะ

4. ยืนชิ

5. ระยะทางมานานายชาญ

6. พระมีงางาม

7. ทำพิธีคนธง

8. มัวธัมมลม

9. ราคายางนายชาญ

10. ชาวนา (คนทำนา) พา (นำ) นายชาญมา

11. มีชัยน

12. ชายนำพื้นมา

13. คืน, คน, นาง, พึง, ลม, ลา

14. ชาวลาว (คนลาว), วิธี, คำ, วา, ฮา, พระ

15. นาน, นะ, ชาม, ภาระ, ยาง, วา

16. ความงง, ความงาม, ช่า, ชี, ระยะทาง, วิชา,

C) 1. คำ, ชาม, ทำ, นิภา, พระ, พื้น, มี, ยา, ยาง, ยืน, ระยะทาง, ราคา, ลาว, ลืม, วิธี.

2. งาน, ทำ, นะ, นา, นาน, นำ, พา, พิธี, พึง, ภาระ, ลม, ลา, วา, วาง, ฮา.

3. นาง, นางนิภา, นาย, นายชาญ, นายวิชา, พระ, พา, พามา, พิธี, พึง, พื้น, ภาระ

** **Lesson 10**

A) 1. The lawyer has capital.

2. In Lampoon there are some rice-farmers.

3. Mr. Chan should work in place of Mr. Wicha.

4. Come in (on) time, please!

5. throw, should, why, substitute, for, lawyer, capital.

B) 1. ทนายความพึ่งมา

2. นายชาญโยนฆาม

3. นายวิชามีเวลาทำงานแทนนางนิภา

4. ทุน, ลำพูน, ทันเวลา, พึ่ง, ใน, ทำไม

C) 1. ทนายความ, ทันเวลา, ทุน, แทน, ลำพูน, เวลา.

2. คน, ควร, คำนำ, ทำไม, นาย, ใน, พระ, โยน.

3. งาน, ทาง, ทำงาน, ทำนา, ทุน, พิธี, ระยะทาง.

** Lesson 11

A) 1. Khun Chan has a rice-farm in Nakawn Panom.

2. (There was) someone (who) brought the bell.

3. (There are some) workers (who) have come to develop the region.

4. The rice-farmer invited Khun Wicha to come and look over the buffalo.

5. military region, win, compliment, milk, city, who

B) 1. คุณชาญ มานครพนมนะ

2. มีคนงานชมควาย

3. มีเณร, พระ, ชี

4. ทนายความชนะคุณ

5. ชวนนางนิภามานครพนมนะ

6. มณฑล, ภาค, คำชม, นคร, ระฆัง, ใคร.

C) 1. คนงาน, ชนะ, นคร, นม, มณฑล, ระฆัง.

2. คุณ, ชม, ชวน, เณร, นครพนม, ภาค.

3. ควาย, คำชม, คุณ, ใคร, ชี, พระ,

** **Lesson 12**

1. Please come back wtth Khun Prani.
2. What ministry will you go to (are you going to)?
3. The price is eight baht.
4. Khun Wicha is very happy.
5. Good-hearted people have compassion.
6. There is a lot of development.
7. Go and tell Mrs. Nipa.
8. May be Khun Chan will go a long distance (far away).
9. The farmer has eight buffalos.
10. Eight rebels have returned.
11. There is a ministerial regulation.
12. The rice-farmer beat the buffalo a long time.
13. Who will go to Nakawn Panom?
14. Go and tell the workers.
15. Khun Chana praised Khun Prani.

** **Lesson 13**

1. I will return to my country.
2. Khun Chan works with (for) the Thai government.
3. I will go (am going) to Silom Road.
4. I had a good dream (I dreamed very well).
5. The tax is ten baht.
6. Go with me to see Khun Nipa, please.
7. Will you go (Are you going)?
8. Do you have three baht?
9. Six buffalos? (Six buffalos, you say?)
10. Two men came to see you.

** **Lesson 14**

    1. Did Khun Wicha kick him?

    2. Thailand has many islands.

    3. A tiger came (walked here) to see you.

    4. I am very sorry.

    5. Khun Chana has a wife.

    6. Let's go to the Sorn Daeng, okay?   (Would it be good for us to go to the Sorn Daeng together?)

    7. What company does he work for?   (At what company does he work?)

    8. The tiger tortured the buffalo.

    9. Perhaps (Maybe) it will be very dirty (soiled).

   10. Who belched?

   11. English or Thai?   (The English language or the Thai language?)

RAPID THAI

LESSON 1

REFERENCE TABLE # 1

Thai Consonant, Name, and Thai Alphabetical Order	English Sound	Thai vowel, sound, and position in writing	EXAMPLE OF WORD CONSTRUCTION		
			Thai	Phonetics	Meaning
ค KAW – 4	**K**	อ AW – after	คอ	KAW	neck (noun)
ด DAW – 20	**D**	◌ุ OO-underneath	ดุ	DOO	look, look at
ท TAW – 23	**T**	เ – EH – before	เท	TEH	pour (verb)
น NAW – 25	**N**	– า AH – after	นา	NAH	rice field
ม MAW – 33	**M**	◌ี EE - above	มี	MEE	have, has, there is, there are
ย YAW – 34	**Y**	–าย AI – after	ยาย	YAI	maternal grand-mother

EXERCISES

A) Translate to English.

    1. ยายมีนา

    2. ดูยายเท

    3. ดูคอยาย

B) Give the names of the following consonants:—

    น, ท, ค, ม, ย, ต

C) Give the sounds of the following vowels:—

    เ, ◌ุ, อ, ◌ี, าย, า

D) Arrange the following consonants in Thai alphabetical

order:—   ม, ย, ค, ต, ท, น

E) Write the following vowel sounds in the correct place
(after, above, before, or underneath) in relation to the consonant
given in each case:—

    1. Consonant——น;   vowel——เ

    2. Consonant——ค;   vowel——าย

    3. Consonant——ย;   vowel——◌ี

    4. Consonant——ค;   vowel——◌ุ

    5. Consonant——ม;   vowel——า

    6. Consonant——ท;   vowel——อ

(Answers to the Exercises of Lesson 1)   (See "Notes".)

A) 1. Grandmother has (a) rice field.

2. Look at grandmother pouring.

3. Look at grandmother's neck.

B) NAW, TAW, KAW, MAW, YAW, DAW

C) EH, OO, AW, EE, AI, AH

D) ก, ค, ท, น, ม, ย

E) 1. เน;   2. คาย;   3. ยฺ;   4. คฺ;   5. มา;   6. ทอ

Notes.   (For Exercise "A".)

1)   The adjective or article "a" need not be translated in Thai.

2)   The basic from of a Thai verb does not change; the same form is used for all tenses and constructions, with the meaning being made clear by helping words and the context.

3)   Possession in Thai may be shown simply by placing what is possessed before the possessor.

LESSON 2

REFERENCE TABLE ǂ 2

Thai Consonant, Name, and Thai Alphabetical Order	English Sound	Thai vowel, sound, and position in writing	EXAMPLE OF WORD CONSTRUCTION		
			Thai	Phonetics	Meaning
ค (Lesson 1)	Lesson 1	OH! (unwritten — understood — between 2 consonants)	คน	KOH!N	1) person, people 2) stir (verb)
ข (r)KAW—2	K	อ (Lesson 1)	ขอ	(r)KAW	ask for ask for something, ask to do something
จ JAW—8	J	า (Lesson 1)	จาน	JAHN	dish, plate
ฉ (r)CHAW—9	CH	◌ั AH!-between 2 consonants	ฉัน	(r)CHAH!N	I, me (mostly for female speakers)
ผ (r)PAW—28	P	OH! (unwritten—understood — between 2 consonants)	ผม	(r)POH!M	1) I, me (mostly for male speakers 2) hair (of the head)
พ PAW—30	P	อ (Lesson 1)	พอ	PAW	enough

NOTES ON REFERENCE TABLE # 2

1) The exclamation point in our phonetics indicates a brief-emphatic vowel sound as opposed to a vowel sound of normal duration. It is wise that you understand from the beginning of your study of Thai that Thai vowels are divided into two main groups: **brief-emphatic vowels** (indicated by an exclamation point in our phonetics) and **normal vowels** (sometimes called "long vowels", but this is a misnomer). To pronounce the Thai word "คน — KOH!N" correctly, simply say it quickly and emphatically (but without any rising or falling of the voice, for this word has a NORMAL TONE).

2) A small "r" in parentheses before a syllable (or a one-syllable word) indicates that the following syllable has a RISING TONE. The rising tone is very easy to render: simply begin the syllable in a low tone and end it in a higher tone of voice. (Although many tones in Thai are not enunciated clearly in everyday conversation, the rising-toned syllables usually are; that is one reason we wish to introduce you to Thai tones from the beginning. In any case, don't worry for fear that you wont't be able to use tones in speaking Thai, and don't think you are "tone deaf". Thai tones are not as difficult as you may have imagined or heard.)

3) You can see by now that Thai vowels are written in various positions in relation to the consonants with which they are used. This may be confusing to you at first, if you are used to seeing vowels always coming after the consonants with which they are used (as most people from the Western part of the world are). However, you will soon agree, we believe, that the Thai language is easy to read once you learn the system; one particularly good thing about it is that the vowel sounds are standardized and do not vary from word to word (as they do in some languages, especially English).

4) There is only one basic form for all Thai letters (both vowels and consonants); no matter how large or small a letter may be, and no matter whether it is printed or written by hand, the basic

form never changes.   However, it is true that individuals have
their own handwriting styles (some of which are indeed difficult
to read!) and that letters are sometimes changed around a bit in
the printed form in order to look more attractive or interesting;
nevertheless, you will always be able to know which letter is which
if you have learned the basic form of it well.

SUMMARY OF THAI LETTERS
COVERED UP TO DATE

1) **Summary of consonants**. (Thai vowels and Thai consonants
are considered separately because they are governed by different
rules, as you will see gradually.)

A.   ข [(r) KAW-2)] (Remember that the number after the
phonetic name of the consonant indicates the alphabetical order of
the consonant in the official Thai alphabet of 44 consonants.   It
is a good thing to try to remember this alphabetical order along
with the consonant itself, as this will help you greatly when you
start looking up words in a Thai dictionary.)

B.   ค (KAW—4)

C.   จ (JAW—8)

D.   ฉ [(r) CHAW—9)]

E.   ด (DAW—20)

F.   ท (TAW—23)

G.   น (NAW—25)

H.   ผ [(r) PAW—28)]

I.   พ (PAW—30)

J.   ม (MAW—33)

K.   ย (YAW—34)

2) **Summary of vowels (both written and unwritten)** (An example is given in each case to illustrate the vowels in words.)

A) **Unwritten but understood.**

OH! (between two consonants, which are usually the only two consonants of that syllable) (คน)

B) **Written.** (Do not concern yourself with the alphabetical order of vowels at this point, as this order is more difficult to learn than the consonantal order; the consonantal alphabetical order is more important anyway.

1. ˇ $\left(\text{AH!--between 2 consonants}\right)$ $\left(ฉัน\right)$

2. า $\left(\text{AH--after a consonant}\right)$ $\left(นา\right)$

3. าย $\left(\text{AI--after a consonant}\right)$ $\left(ยาย\right)$

4. ◌̂ $\left(\text{EE--above a consonant}\right)$ $\left(มี\right)$

5. ◌ุ $\left(\text{OO--underneath a consonant}\right)$ $\left(ดู\right)$

6. เ $\left(\text{EH--before a consonant}\right)$ $\left(เท\right)$

7. อ $\left(\text{AW--after a consonant}\right)$ $\left(คอ\right)$

EXERCISES

(Based on Lessons 1 and 2)

A) Translate to English.

1. ฉันมีจาน

2. ผมขอดู

3. มีคนพอ

4. ฉันขอเท

5. ยายขอจาน

B) Give the names of the following consonants:–

ผ, จ, ค, ย, พ, บ, ก, ม, น, ฉ, ท

C) Give the sounds of the following vowels:–

เ, ˇ, อ, (คน), า, ˆ, ุ, าย

D) Arrange the following consonants in Thai alphabetical

oder:– ฉ, จ, ย, บ, ผ, ค, พ, ก, ม, น, ท

E) Write the following vowel sounds in the correct place
(after, above, before, underneath or between) in relation to the
consonant(s) given in each case:–

    1. Consonant––ผ; vowel––ˆ

    2. Consonant––จ; vowel––า

    3. Consonant––ค; vowel––าย

    4. Consonants––นย: vowel––ˇ

    5. Consonant––ท: vowel––อ

(Answers to the Exercises of Lesson 2)

    A) 1. I have (a) plate. ("I" here is probably feminine.)

        2. I beg to see. (Let me see.) ("I" here is masculine.)

        3. There are enough people.

        4. I beg to pour (it). (Let me pour it.) ("It" is often
omitted in Thai; in this case "it" might be "tea".)

        5. Grandmother asks (asked, has asked) for (a) plate.

    B) (r) PAW, JAW, DAW, YAW, PAW, (r) KAW, KAW,
MAW, NAW, (r) CHAW, TAW.

    C) EH, AH!, AW, OH! (unwritten but understood), AH,
EE, OO, AI

    D) บ, ค, จ, ฉ, ค, ฑ, น, ผ, พ, ม, ย

    E) 1. ผี; 2. จา; 3. คาย; 4. นัย; 5. ทอ

LESSON 3

ADDITIONAL VOCABULARY

STOP! Before you give up learning Thai in disgust, please give us a chance to show you that it is not as difficult and time-consuming as it may appear. Our publisher has said—and we agree with him—that if one spends only 15-30 minutes on each of our lessons and learns a basic vocabulary of only about 200 words, then he can speak enough Thai to make himself understood and can travel around Thailand without any trouble.

Therefore, using only the Thai letters already taught you in Lessons 1 and 2, we will give you in this Lesson the 12 words already introduced, plus 13 new words.

AT THE END OF THIS LESSON, WE ARE CONFIDENT THAT YOU WILL BE ABLE TO USE 25 THAI WORDS WELL. IF OUR PUBLISHER IS CORRECT, THAT LEAVES ONLY 175 WORDS TO GO IN ORDER TO HAVE A BASIC VOCABULARY. (Please stay with us, then, for a few more lessons, if for no other reason than to prove whether our publisher is right or wrong!)

I. Alphabetical summary of vocabulary up-to-date (including some new, additional meanings)

THAI	PHONETICS	MEANING
1. ขอ	(r)KAW	ask for, ask for something, ask to do something
2. คน	KOH!N	(1) person, people (2) stir (verb)
3. คอ	KAW	neck (noun)
4. จาน	JAHN	dish, plate
5. ฉัน	(r)CHAH!N	I, me (mostly for female speakers)

THAI	PHONETICS	MEANING
6. ดู	DOO	look, look at
7. เท	TEH	pour
8. นา	NAH	rice field
9. ผม	(r)POH!M	(1) I, me (mostly for male speakers) (2) hair (of the head)
10. พอ	PAW	enough, as soon as
11. มี	MEE	have, has, there is, there are
12. ยาย	YAI	maternal grandmother

II. Easy Grammatical Points about the Preceding 12 Words.

A) The verb ขอ is often used without any subject.   In such cases, however, the subject is understood.

Example :–   ขอจาน

(r)KAW JAHN

(I) ask for a plate.   (=Please give me a plate. The pronoun "I" is understood and is not expressed.)

B) Thus, the verb ขอ may often be transtated as "please give...." or "Let me....".

1. ขอคน

(r)KAW KOH!N

Please give me somebody.

2. ขอดู

(r)KAW DOO

Let me see.

C) There are many more personal pronouns used in Thai than in English.   In Thai, the personal pronoun to use normally depends on the status of the speaker, his relationship to the person spoken to, and the circumstances at hand.   However, this is not as confusing as it may sound.   In most cases, you may safely use ผม for "I" if you are a male, and ฉัน for "I" if you are a female.

D) Thai grammar is simple and uncomplicated in everyday usage, since there are no verb conjugations or separate tense forms, no singular and plural forms for nouns, no masculine and feminine forms for nouns (as in some languages), etc. For our present purposes in learning Thai easily and rapidly, in order to use it in everyday life or as a prelude to a more serious study, we can therefore say that Thai grammar is very easy. However, this does not mean that Thai or Thai grammar on a higher level is easy; on the contrary, the Thai language is one on which a person could easily spend a lifetime of study, if he had the time and the inclination to do so.

III. **Some new words (in Thai alphabetical order) using the Thai letters you have already learned.**

Thai	Phonetics	Meaning
1. ขน	(r) KOH!N	hair (of the body or of an animal)
2. ขม	(r)KOH!M	bitter (in taste)
3. ขา	(r)KAH	leg
4. ขาย	(r)KAI	sell (verb)
5. คม	KOH!M	sharp
6. คีม	KEEM	tongs, pliers
7. จน	JOH!N	(1) poor; 2) until
8. จาม	JAHM	sneeze (verb)
9. จีน	JEEN	Chinese, Chinese people
10 ดม	DOH!M	sniff, smell (verb)
11. ดี	DEE	good, well
12. มา	MAH	come
13. ผี	(r)PEE	ghost (noun)

IV. **Easy Grammatical Points about the Preceding New 13 Words.**

A) Notice how the rising tone distinguishes between the two words คน and ขน. (In such cases as these, it is important to distinguish between the tones.   However, you will see that the different tones are not always clearly enunciated in everyday speech. This means, for a foreigner learning Thai, that he can make many mistakes in tones and still be clearly understood by a native speaker of Thai.   Nevertheless, it is best to try to distinguish between tones if you can, in such important cases especially as these two words คน and ขน.)

B)   It is not necessary to have a "be" verb in Thai when an adjective describes a noun or pronoun.   Thus, the adjective merely comes after the noun or pronoun, and a "be" verb is understood.

Example :— ผมจน

(r)POH!M JOH!N

I (am) poor.

C)   คนจีน = Chinese people (the adjective usually comes after the noun it modifies).

EXERCISES

A)   **Translate to English**

1. คิมฉันดี

2. ผมขายดี

3. มีผมมา

4. มีคนพอ

5. ยายดมจาน

6. คนมีขนขา

7. ขอดูคนจีน

8. มีคนมาดูนาฉัน

9. ผมขายนาผม

10. มีคนจีนจาม

B) **Translate to Thai** (You should begin trying to write Thai words yourself, if you have the time. However, if you are in too big of a hurry, you can of course eliminate this exercise. You can learn to read Thai well without learning to write it also, but writing the words down yourself will help fix them in your memory.)

1. I am selling tongs. (masculine "I"; although there is a way to express the continuous or progressive tenses in Thai, you need use only the normal form of the verb "sell" in this case).

2. There is (a) Chinese person (who) has come. (Words in parentheses need not be translated.)

3. My plates (are) good. (Make "my" feminine here.)

4. Let me see (some) good tongs. ("let me" may be translated with one verb, as explained in Lesson 3.)

(Answers)

A) 1. My tongs are good.
    2. I am selling well.
    3. A ghost has come.
    4. There are enough people.
    5. Grandmother smells of the plate.
    6. People have hairs on their legs.
    7. Let me see the poor people.
    8. Someone has come to see my rice field.
    9. I am selling (have sold) my rice field.
    10. A Chinese person sneezed.

B) 1. ผมขายคีม   2. มีคนจีนมา

    3. จานฉันดี   4. ขอดูคีมดี

LESSON 4

THE THAI ALPHABET
(Part One)

NOTE. In this lesson we begin an orderly but gradual introduction of all the Thai alphabet, IN THAI ALPHABETICAL ORDER. You should not try to memorize all these from the beginning, however. The best thing to do is to be able to use our REFERENCE TABLES to help you do our exercises. Thus, you will learn the Thai alphabet by USING it, and this is generally the best way to learn anything. (You have already used some of these Thai letters in our previous lessons.)

REFERENCE TABLE 3
CONSONANTS (Part One)

Note. A few Thai consonants are no longer used in normal Thai writing; therefore, these obsolete Thai consonants will not be included in these lists.)

Thai Consonant	Numerical Order in Regular Thai Alphabet	English Equivalent	
		Initial	Final
ก	1	G	K
ข	2	K	K
ค	4 (# 3 is obsolete)	K	K
ฆ	6 (# 5 is obsolete)	K	K
ง	7	NG	NG
จ	8	J	T
ฉ	9	CH	T
ช	10	CH	T

NOTES.

1) The total number of consonants in the Thai alphabet is 44. However, some of these are obsolete and some are not used very much.

2) Notice that some consonants have one sound at the beginning of a syllable but another one at the end.

3) The "NG" sound coming at the beginning of a syllable is difficult for most foreign speakers of Thai at first, but this sound can easily be made by anyone with some practice.

4) There is much disagreement about transliteration of Thai letters into English (or Roman) letters.   Thus, you are likely to see "K" for "ก" (instead of our "G"), "KH" for "ข" and "ค" (instead of our "K"), "CH" for "จ" (instead of our "J"), etc. However, we believe you will find that our own phonetics are as accurate as possible in regard to the true Thai sounds.

REFERENCE TABLE 4
VOWELS (Part One)

NOTE. In the Thai alphabet, consonants and vowels are considered separately because they are governed by different rules. The alphabetical order for consonants is clear, orderly, and unmistakable; however, the alphabetical order for vowels is not so orderly and is sometimes rather confusing. In any event, we try to list vowels in alphabetical order insofar as possible (in order gradually to accustom you to this order, which will be very useful for you to have well in mind when you eventually start using Thai dictionaries.)   (However, we leave until the last the unwritten vowels and the consonants sometimes used as vowels, since these types of vowels are the most confusing for beginners in Thai; and we omit altogether a few very rare vowels.)   Notice that Thai vowels are written in a number of positions in relation to the consonant or consonants with which they are used, but the position of a certain vowel is fixed and unchangeable.

Thai Vowel	Location in relation to Consonants(s) with which used	English equivalent
◌ะ	after	AH!
◌ั	between and above 2 consonants of the same syllable	AH!
า	after	AH
°า	after	AH!M
◌ิ	above	EE!
◌ี	above	EE

NOTE. Remember that our exclamation point in phonetics indicates a brief-emphatic vowel sound as opposed to a vowel sound of normal duration. (For examples of these vowels used in words, see the "Vocabulary" Section following this section on vowels. You should be able to recognize the consonants and vowels of which a certain word is composed and know where to find these letters in our REFERENCE TABLES.)

VOCABULARY SECTION

NOTE. In the first three lessons, we introduced you to 25 Thai words and told you our objective is to give you—first of all—a basic vocabulary of 200 words in only 15-30 minutes of your time for each of these lessons. In this lesson we review for you the 25 words already introduced and give you 15 useful new words (making use, of course, only of the Thai letters already explained and listed in the REFERENCE TABLES up to now). Please see our preceding lessons for simple grammatical points concerning these words. Do not waste your time trying to memorize these words; your time would be better spent trying to use them correctly in the exercises of this lesson or in speaking them to someone. Learn through using!

Word List including Words Previously Introduced
(in Thai alphabetical order)

THAI	PHONETICS	TRANSLATION(S)
1. กัน	GAH!N	to each other, with each other (shows mutuality)
2. กิน	GEE!N	eat, consume (common, everyday verb)
3. ขน	(r)KOH!N	hair (of the body or of an animal)
4. ขม	(r)KOH!M	bitter (in taste)
5. ขยาย	KAH!-(r)YAI	enlarge, expand (verb)
6. ขอ	(r)KAW	ask for, ask for something, ask to do something
7. ของ	(r)KAWNG	of, belonging to (used mostly to show possession)
8. ขา	(r)KAH	leg
9. ขาย	(r)KAI	sell (verb)
10. คน	KOH!N	(1) person, people: (2) stir (verb)
11. คม	KOH!M	sharp
12. คอ	KAW	neck (verb)
13. คอย	KAWY	wait (verb)
14. คำ	KAH!M	word (noun)
15. คิด	KEE!T	think
16. คิดดู	KEE!T DOO	thing something over
17. คิม	KEEM	tongs, pliers

THAI	PHONETICS	TRANSLATION(S)
18. งาน	NGAHN	work (noun)
19. จง	JOH!NG	must (helping verb)
20. จน	JOH!N	(1) poor; (2) until
21. จะ	JAH!	shall, will (helping verb)
22. จาน	JAHN	dish, plate
23. จาม	JAHM	sneeze (verb)
24. จีน	JEEN	Chinese, Chinese people
25. ฉัน	(r)CHAH!N	I, me (mostly for female speakers)
26. ชน	CHOH!N	run into, bump into (verb)
27. ชนะ	CHAH!-NAH!	win (verb)
28. ดม	DOH!M	sniff, smell (verb)
29. ดี	DEE	good, well
30. ดู	DOO	look, look at
31. ทำ	TAH!M	do, make
32. ทำงาน	TAH!M-NGAHN	work (verb)
33. เท	TEH	pour (verb)
34. นา	NAH	rice field
35. ผม	(r)POH!M	(1) I, me (mostly for male speakers); 2) hair (of head)
36. พอ	PAW	enough as soon as
37. ผี	(r)PEE	ghost (noun)
38. มา	MAH	come
39. มี	MEE	have, has, there is, there are
40. ยาย	YAI	maternal grandmother

EXERCISES

Translate into English

1. จงทำงานพอดี

2. นาของฉันมีผี

3. ยายจะคอยผม

4. ฉันชนขาของคนจีน

5. จงดีกัน มาทำงานกัน

6. คนจีนกินดี

7. พอฉันดมดู ฉันจาม

8. จงมีคำดี

9. ฉันจะคิดดู

10. พอผมชนะ ผมจะมาขยายงาน

Note. We agree that our Thai's not so good, but we're trying to do the best we can with 40 words.

(Answers)

1. You must do your work well enough. ("you" and "your" are understood)
2. My rice farm has a ghost on it.
3. Grandmother will wait for me.
4. I ran into the Chinaman's leg.
5. You must be good to each other (get along well); come and work together.
6. Chinese people eat well.
7. As soon as I sniffed, I sneezed.
8. You must have good words.
9. I will think it over.
10. As soon as I win, I will come to expand the work.

Note. You should now know 40 useful Thai words!

LESSON 5

THE THAI ALPHABET (Part Two)

REFERENCE TABLE 5

CONSONANTS (Part Two)

Thai Consonant	Numerical Order in Regular Thai Alphabet	English Equivalent	
		Initial	Final
ซ	11	S	--
ญ	13 (ฌ 12 is too rare to be worth mentioning here)	Y	N
ฎ	13 (rare)	D	T
ฏ	15 (rather rare)	DT	T
ฐ	16 (rather rare)	T	T
ณ	19 (ฑ 17 & 18 are too rare to be worth mentioning at this time)	N	N
ด	20	D	T
ต	21	DT	T

NOTES.

1) Perhaps you have already noticed that the same consonant sound in Thai may be expressed by more than one consonant, in some cases. There are many reasons for having such "duplicate" consonants, but these reasons are too detailed to worry about now. In any event, you can no doubt now partially understand why there are so many consonants (44) in the Thai alphabet.

2) The "DT" sound of "ฏ" and "ต" (at the beginning of a syllable) is a difficult one for most Westerners to make. It is

best learned by imitation, but what it really amounts to is a sort of forced and explosive "T" sound (with the tongue first pressed against the back of the upper teeth and then released quickly, making a more forced and more explosive sound than we make for normal "D" and "T" sounds). If you know Chinese, then this sound will be easy for you since it is used in Chinese also.

3) You have already seen that some consonants have a rising sound in their name (such as "(r) KAW﹣﹣ย") and often cause a rising tone in a syllable (such as "(r) KAW﹣﹣ขอ"). Another example of such a "rising consonant" (actually called "high-class consonants") is "ฐ".

REFERENCE TABLE 6
VOWELS (Part Two)

Thai Vowel	Location in Relation to Consonant(s) with which used	English Equivalent
◌ึ	above	EU!
◌ื	above	EU
◌ุ	underneath	OO!
◌ู	underneath	OO
เ	preceding	EH
เ—า	preceding and after $\left(2 \text{ parts}\right)$	AO!

NOTES.

1) The vowel sounds in Thai are mostly easy to imitate for Westerners; however, the vowel sound of "EU﹣﹣ึ" is an exception. This sound is somewhat like the vowel sound in "good", but if you see someone pronounce it correctly you will notice that he stretches his lips when saying "ึ".

2) Notice again the differences between the normal-duration vowel sounds (such as EU, OO, EH) and the brief-emphatic vowel sounds (such as EU!, OO!, and AO!). There is nothing really difficult about making this differentiation in the length of vowel sounds, but it is admittedly strange at first to most Westerners. However, the same as with tones, a vowel sound given the wrong time-duration can still be understood in most cases. Nevertheless, it is also true that a vowel sound mispronounced in this way could conceivably lead to a misunderstanding (just as the wrong tone may sometimes do the same thing), due to the fact that meanings of words in Thai vary according to the tone and vowel-sound used.

VOCABULARY SECTION

NOTE. We have already given you a total of 40 basic Thai words, using only the consonants and vowels already introduced. In this lesson we now propose to give you 20 additional useful Thai words, making use primarily of the consonants and vowels in the REFERENCE TABLES of this lesson. However, we will of course also use some consonants and vowels that have been introduced in previous lessons.

WORD LIST (in Thai alphabetical order)

THAI	PHONETICS	TRANSLATIONS
1. กฎ	GOH!T	rule, regulation
2. กันยายน	GA!N-YAH-YO!HN	September
3. ขณะ	KAH!-NAH!	a certain time, at a certain time
4. ขัง	$\left(r\right)$KAH!NG	shut up, lock in, imprison
5. ขัด	KAH!T	polish, shine $\left(\text{verb}\right)$

THAI	PHONETICS	TRANSLATIONS
6. ขัน	(r)KAH!N	amusing, funny
7. ขาด	KAHT	torn, missing, absent, to lack
8. ขีด	KEET	draw a line, scratch something against something else (as a match)
9. เขา	(r)KAO!	he, she, him, her
10. คณะ	KA!-NAH	group, party (of persons)
11. คดี	KAH!-DEE	case, suit (in court)
12. คืน	KEUN	night (noun); return (verb)
13. คือ	KEU	that is, that is to say (connecting word); (also may mean "be" in some cases)
14. คุณ	KOON!	you (informal but polite); (also used politely as a prefix to a person's first name, either when speaking to him or about him)
15. จึง	JEU!NG	therefore (connecting word); in order to, then
16. ชาติ	CHAHT	nation, nationality (also may mean "life" in certain cases)
17. ชิ	SEE!	(imperative word used at the end of commands)

THAI	PHONETICS	TRANSLATIONS
18. ญาติ	YAHT	relative(s) $(persons)$
19. ฐานะ	(r)TAH-NAH	status, circumstances $(มีฐานะดี$ = to be well off, to be someone of means$)$
20. นางนาฏ	NAHNG-NAHT	a beautiful young woman, such as an actress; นาง alone means "woman". $($NOTES. This expression is used very little and has been given only to illustrate the use of the rather rare consonant "ฏ" in a word.$)$

Notes. 1) Note the similar-appearing pronunciation in our phonetics for the words "บณะ" and "คณะ". Actually, there is a tonal difference, as you will learn in later studies.

2) Some of the words you have learned so far will be rather difficult to use correctly in the following exercises, since they are normally used with other accompanying words. Therefore, please be patient with our sometimes "incomplete" Thai construction, due to the fact that we have not introduced you to a larger vocabulary.

EXERCISES

Translate into English

1. จงมีกฎดีจึงจะทำงานดี

2. คอยชิ! กันยายนฉันจะไปดู

3. บณะทำงาน จงทำดี

4. คณะของเขาขาดงานทำ จึงมาดูงานของผม

5. ขณะจะขังเขา คุณจามพอดี

6. ขัดคีมของเขาซิ!

7. งานของคณะของเขา ขันดี

8. คุณทำขีดพอดี

9. เขาจะคืนคดี คือญาติของเขามีฐานะดี

10. ฐานะของชาติดี

Notes. We naturally confine the vocabulary in these exercises to the number of words that have been introduced to you up-to-date. The current total vocabulary is 60 words.

(Answers)

1. You (One) must have good regulations; then you can do good work.
2. Wait! (In) September I'll go see.
3. While working, (you) must do (it) well.
4. His group lacked work to do; therefore, (they) came to see my work.
5. At the time (they) were about to lock him up, you sneezed at that very moment. ("พอดี"="at that very moment.")
6. Polish his tongs!
7. The work of his group is very amusing. ("ดี" can also mean "very".)
8. You made the line (drew the line) just right.
9. He will return the case; that is, his relatives are well off.
10. The status of the nation is good.